The Arch of Kerguelen

The Arch of Kerguelen
Voyage to the Islands of Desolation

JEAN-PAUL KAUFFMANN

Translated from the French by Patricia Clancy

Four Walls Eight Windows
New York/London

Published in the United States by
Four Walls Eight Windows
39 West 14th Street
New York, NY 10011
http://www.4w8w.com

UK offices:
Four Walls Eight Windows/Turnaround
Unit 3 Olympia Trading Estate
Coburg Road, Wood Green
London N22 6TZ

First printing October 2000.
First published by Flammarion in France in 1993.

Library of Congress Cataloging-in-Publication Data:
Kauffmann, Jean-Paul.
[Arche des Kerguelen. English]
The arch of Kerguelen: voyage to the islands of Desolation/by Jean-Paul Kauffmann; translated by Patricia Clancy.
p. cm.
ISBN 1-56858-168-8
1. Kerguelen Islands—Description and travel. I. Clancy, P. A. II. Title.
DS349.9.K47 K3813 2000
916.9'9—dc21   00-057839

Printed in the United States
10   9   8   7   6   5   4   3   2   1

For Joëlle

"Then the temple of God was opened in heaven, and the ark of His covenant was seen in His temple. And there were lightnings, noises, thunderings, an earthquake, and great hail."

Revelation, XI, 19

Table of Contents

Acknowledgments

I would particularly like to thank Gracie Delépine, Alain Boulaire, Lieutenant-Colonel Pierre Couesnon, and Denis Tillinac for their invaluable help.

I would also like to express my gratitude to Claude Baravian, Olivier Brun, Michel Cantal-Dupart, Philippe Caparroy, Admiral Claude Corbier, Patrick Davaine, Bernard Duboys de Lavigerie; to Captaine Étienne Guillier, Jean-François Kahn, Damien Levallois, Gabriel Picot, Georges Polian, Maurice Recq, Viviane Richard, Max Schmid, Raphaël Sorin, Wenni Wellsandt; to the Office of the French Southern and Antarctic Territories (TAAF), which made this voyage possible, and also to the members of the fortieth and forty-first missions to the Kerguelens who made me welcome.

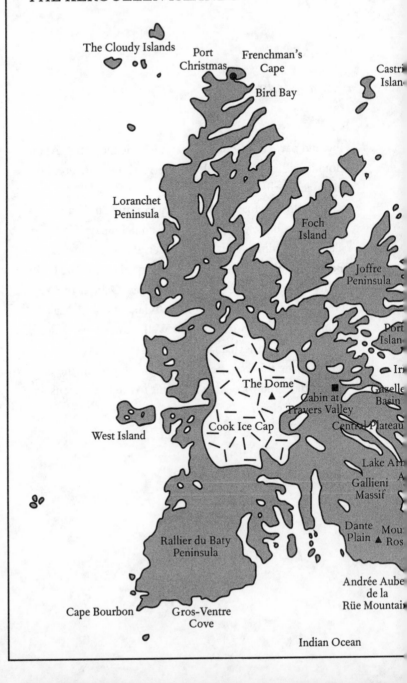

THE KERGUELEN ISLANDS

The Cloudy Islands

Port Christmas

Frenchman's Cape

Castri Islan

Bird Bay

Loranchet Peninsula

Foch Island

Joffre Peninsula

Port Islan

Ir

The Dome

Gazelle Basin

Cabin at Travers Valley

Cook Ice Cap

Central Plateau

West Island

Lake Ar

Gallieni Massif

A

Dante Plain

Mou Ros

Rallier du Baty Peninsula

Andrée Aube de la Rüe Mountai

Cape Bourbon

Gros-Ventre Cove

Indian Ocean

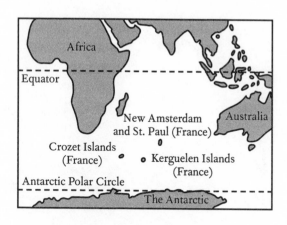

Africa

Equator

New Amsterdam
and St. Paul (France)

Australia

Crozet Islands
(France)

Kerguelen Islands
(France)

Antarctic Polar Circle

The Antarctic

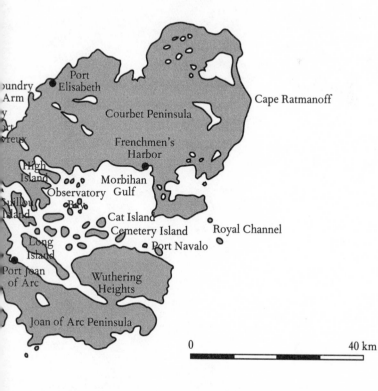

Port
Elisabeth

oundry
Arm

Courbet Peninsula

Cape Ratmanoff

ort
vreux

Frenchmen's
Harbor

High
Island

Morbihan
Gulf

Observatory

kilou
land

Cat Island

Cemetery Island

Royal Channel

Long
Island

Port Navalo

Port Joan
of Arc

Wuthering
Heights

Joan of Arc Peninsula

0   40 km

PART ONE

"His Majesty seemed satisfied..."

"When you were a child gazing at one of those pages in your atlas filled with the most blue, surely you dreamed, like me, of that Antarctic land, remote yet still ours and French, Kerguelen."

Valéry Larbaud
The Governor of Kerguelen

I've dreamed of Kerguelen all my life. Sitting propped up against the sacks of wheat in my father's bakery, I saw myself as Jim Hawkins, the young hero of *Treasure Island*. I kept watch for danger behind the *stockade*, a word that seemed all the more exotic as I didn't know then it was a fort. One day, hidden away there among the sacks while my father, like Vulcan, was pulling the burning sticks of firewood from the oven and throwing them into the metal bin, while I was reading *Spirou*, I came across the adventures of the Chevalier de Kerguelen, told by one "Uncle Paul." This Breton sailor had left France at the end of Louis XV's reign to discover Eldorado, but all he found was a desolate land that so offended him he refused to set foot on it. When he returned, he was tried and thrown in prison.

The old atlas I had then didn't mention these mysterious islands and I'd always thought they were Breton. I was sure something was being hidden from me. What crime had Kerguelen committed?

I loved the strange sound of his name from the very beginning. He was said to have given France a wild, barren land called Desolation. But I learned later that this archipelago is inhabited by fascinating animals and that it was as green as the meadows of his native Brittany. I was amazed at the thought that this faraway continent was part of France. I also had the feeling there was a mystery to it. From then on, I was aware that a secret buried deep within a man's life had been passed on to the land he had discovered.

I spent a lot of time in libraries, examined old papers, and untied the string around ancient boxes, holding my breath in anticipation. The further I went, the more the mystery eluded me, like the message left in the bottle near the Arched Rock of Kerguelen by Edgar Allen Poe's Captain Guy. In *The Narrative of A. Gordon Pym*, where several episodes take place on Desolation Island, Poe refuses to divulge the secret of the hidden letter.

There are many messages left in bottles in the Kerguelens, but no one has ever found them. I've actually been preparing for this voyage for forty years. I'm going to Christmas Harbor to find that Arched Rock, the Arch of Kerguelen. This gigantic vault, which astounded so many navigators, makes me think of the entrance to a crypt. I fancy that the hidden meaning behind the long-accursed archipelago is concealed there.

I'm happy to confront, of my own free will, the extreme loneliness and the elemental starkness of the hostile natural surroundings. What I am undertaking is no voyage of initiation. There is no Holy Grail to be discovered in this district of the French Southern and Antarctic Territories (TAAF).

Getting to Kerguelen is no easy matter. The Desolation Islands are regarded as the most isolated spot on the globe. Your have to get to Réunion Island and then wait for a boat, the *Marion-Dufresne*, which goes to the French Southern Islands only twice or three times a year. The distance to Kerguelen is one of the last curiosities for a generation that flatters itself it has abolished time and space. No plane can go there. Just as in the time of the whalers called in at Desolation throughout the nineteenth century, these islands reveal themselves little by little, after a long period of forced solitude.

To prepare myself for the ruggedness of the Desolation Islands, for their *astringency*, I allow myself to taste the slightly sickly sweetness of Réunion, the former Île Bourbon. The departure point for Kerguelen in Réunion is called the Port. The simplicity of that all-embracing name with its capital P would indicate that the traveler is invited to make the ultimate discovery of the Ocean, of the Voyage, the Islands. ...I never tire of savoring the heavy fruits, breathing the heady perfumes of the tropics and the softness of the trade winds filled as they are with melodious sound. These syrupy flavors will make me all the more appreciative of the prospective bitterness of Kerguelen.

One day I finally leave the Port, taking only two bags. One contains the books and files I've gathered over the years. The *Marion-Dufresne* is a ship of 390 feet, almost worn out by a hard life in the "roaring forties." It has been servicing the Crozet, Amsterdam, and Kerguelen Islands for well over twenty years. You feel that the salt- and rust-encrusted boat would like to have a breather. Nonetheless, its reflexes still seem to be quite good: the thick, strong frame will hold in the storm. I took an immediate liking to this old wild boar of the sea. This lone ship provides the service of our last shipping line, connecting our most far-flung areas. It brings everything to our southern islands. I found its sense of duty quite touching. It claims to be only a "supply ship," whereas it does

everything: passenger ship, oil tanker, container, or oceanographic ship.

I'm going to have a week's forced idleness on one of the
most deserted and tempestuous seas in the world. But I suspect
that, unlike floating palaces and cruise ships, the *Marion-
Dufresne* will provide the indispensable prelude to getting to
know any unknown country: waiting and boredom.

Isn't having nothing to do the supreme test, even more than
suffering? Whoever can fill the emptiness of his being, when
there is nothing more to occupy it, will survive. He will overcome the cruelest torture: time without limit and without end.
Pain keeps one occupied; the person who suffers sees himself
in his torment. Boredom knows neither variety nor satiety.

I embark with a team of six parachutists based at Réunion.
They are under the command of a young captain and will
undertake a "survival mission" in the Kerguelens. A major is
going with them, who is no stranger to me. I've been corre-
sponding for some time with Major Couesnon. He is the
author of *A Postal History of Kerguelen.* The archipelago is
well-known for the rarity of its covers and the originality of
its stamps. In spite of its modest appearance, this mimeo-
graphed work is still to this day the only serious study on the
archipelago's past.

In the course of my research, I realized that the facts surrounding the discovery of the Kerguelens and its exploration
between 1790 and 1914 explain absolutely nothing. There is no
continuity. Whalers and scientific mission have nearly always
followed one another in ignorance of what went before. I've

sometimes wondered whether they were describing the same country.

There is a bronze plaque engraved with the names of Henry and René Bossière in the hold of the ship. It's packed in strawboard and will be set into the hill at Port aux Français, the base on Kerguelen. Last century, these Le Havre shipowners saved Desolation from oblivion and the British.

The parachutists' wives look sad as they wave to their husbands: they will be away for more than two months. The happiness and excitement of those who are leaving makes those left on the wharf feel miserable. The sympathy expressed by my future traveling companions does not ring true. This obligatory hypocrisy is one of the little cruelties without which travel would lose its appeal. When faced with the joy the deserter feels, the one left behind feels almost guilty.

One by one the hawsers fall into the water and are quickly pulled up on board. The *Marion-Dufresne* is no longer that veteran of the high seas, prostrate along the wharf. It's six o'clock in the evening.... We have just past the Port lighthouse, turning our backs on the Réunion coast. Already no one is paying any attention to the arms still waving in the distance.

I

Dinner is served at seven o'clock. The food is copious, the service carried out in the great tradition of the Transatlantic Line: the maître d'hôtel with epaulettes and the tall Black man in white livery. The *Marion* can take ninety passengers, but on this trip there are only about twenty of us. We are going straight to Kerguelen without stopping at Crozet or Amsterdam, the two other French southern lands.

I make the acquaintance of a Breton who is going to spend a year at Port aux Français. My new friend is brusque, agitated, and also unhappy, falling into long silences interrupted by sudden outbursts of gaiety. Two months ago, on New Year's Day, his wife told him that she was leaving him. "The sky fell on me then, and it's still falling," he sighed. Despair has made him go mad. He admits, not without some pride, that he had smashed up everything in the house. His wife never spoke much. She just confessed to him on the day of the break, "I was suffocating with you. I have to make a clean break." He was a professional fisherman and made a good living. He had bought a nice house, then enlarged it by acquiring the house next door. The breakup lead to another difficulty: he lost his job. "I was too taken up by the whole affair. I lost interest in work." The poor sailor could have taken to drink and brooded over his pain indefinitely. "I made a clean break too by asking to go to the Kerguelens—to forget and think things over. My wife was surprised at my decision. I scored a point."

Most of the men on the ship are bored. They roam around the passageways, have a drink at the bar, then take a siesta. I like this idle, monotonous life. The only leisure activity it has to offer is the aperitif custom and gazing at the ocean. It's a confined existence without any real aim, and for me that is pure truth.

I've discovered the ship's library. The pages have traces of mildew and smell musty. These books probably haven't been opened since the fifties: Louis Bromfield, Rosamond Lehmann, Pierre Benoit. The rather worn cloth bindings bear the names of ships that no longer exist today like the *Pasteur*, a passenger ship of the Messageries Maritimes Steamship Company that is well known to former old hands of the Indochina line.

I settle into a routine very quickly. Late in the afternoon I meet Major Couesnon in the library. We converse about the man, Kerguelen, or the Bossière brothers. The ship's engine makes the paneling and shelves vibrate, sometimes lifting the books and making them collapse like dominos.

On the third day, we catch sight of a ship in the distance. The presence of another vessel in these latitudes, one of the least frequented in the world, causes some brief excitement. What is it doing in a place like this, so far from the usual routes?

"Perhaps it's an ore tanker," an officer says, adding, "That's unusual!"

As soon as it disappeared over the horizon, the mystery ceased to interest anyone. On board ship, the only thing that counts is what can be seen. There's nothing to see: in the end, the sea looks like an abstract, inert surface on which our ship struggles to exist. It can battle the waves, pitch and toss, in short behave as a boat always does, but it still seems to wear itself out in the middle of this empty sea. The word *round*, used to designate every trip that the *Marion* makes between Reunion and the southern ocean islands, has its full meaning here. It's an eternal round, as if there was a beginning but never an end.

A print hanging in the bar tells the sad story of the navigator who gave his name to our ship. Marion Dufresne, who was at Île de France, now called Mauritius, at the same time as Kerguelen, discovered the Crozet Islands on 13 January 1772 at about 47° latitude south. Continuing his route towards the east, he could well have come across Kerguelen too. He reached New Zealand, where he was killed by the Maoris.

I sometimes go out on deck. The color of the sky and the sea is white, as it was yesterday; the same foam streaks the crests of the waves and the ship rises on the same swell. This eternal return of the same thing creates a feeling of indolence, but with brief bursts of energy. The boredom of shipboard life is like no other. It's a slightly heady kind of lassitude where opposite sensations coexist within the same monotony. Despondency and enthusiasm, the old and the new, before and after become confused, blotting out anything that could differentiate one thing from another.

One day we put our watches forward one hour to conform to some imaginary time zone. To the passengers, this seems as arbitrary as you can get: why change watches and clocks when time is no longer of any importance at all?

On another day the temperature becomes cooler. Increasingly bigger and darker waves come over the foredeck. The sailors came into the cabins at dawn to screw down and block up the portholes. Glasses, plates, and dishes are now restricted to the tables in the dining room. The stormy weather has increased our feeling of languid boredom. We hardly leave our cabins. We are incapable of staying on our feet.

The difference between pitching and tossing holds no more mysteries for me. I prefer pitching. The rocking motion back and forth is in the same direction as my bunk, but the sideways jolts are very unpleasant.

The bad weather increases the sense of time also going awry. The word *temps* in French means both weather and time. The confusion between meteorology and duration permitted by the French language now seems logical to me: it's temperature and climate that decide the passing of days and hours.

Once or twice during the day I hazard a sortie outside. The *Marion* is banging hard against the waves that break into foam over the bow. The ship is surrounded by columns of water; they hang in the air for a moment, then roll over and crash against the sides.

One night a sailor comes to tell me that a call from my wife has just come through to the bridge. Everyone is asleep. While the officer of the watch standing next to me looks at the storm outside, I talk to Joëlle by satellite in the gloom. The light on the prow flickers, disappears submerged in the spray, then comes up again. It's the last essential sign of life on this vessel.

Joëlle tells me the news that Saddam Hussein has accepted all the United Nations' resolutions. The Gulf War has ended. In this wild night my wife tells me that she's taking the children to see the film of *Cyrano de Bergerac*. She hands the receiver over to my younger son who says, making fun of me, "Well, Dad. It seems you're having a rough time! Is that an adventure?" He asks me to describe the bad weather and the high seas. I try to give a picture of the foredeck awash with water, the crashing of the waves as they fly up over the hull, the gallant ship struggling in a gale, alone and wretched, against the raging seas.

"Listen to the storm," I say to him, waving the phone above my head. What could he hear from so far away?

"I can hear it!" he exclaims nonetheless. The sound of frying is a fairly good imitation of the sputtering sound the rain makes as it dashes against the window on the bridge.

The weather is colder this morning. Borne along by the anger of the three oceans united, the waves rush forward in the wake of the *Marion* like shouting horsemen. The halyards and lifts are beating in the wind, their sharp creaks and groans becoming more and more piercing. The clouds skim the waves and stay so close to them that the jerking of the boat as it tosses faster and faster has the effect of a bird flushed out of its cover flying off at top speed.

The temperature has fallen sharply in a few hours. We are crossing the subantarctic convergence, the hydrological barrier separating the warm subtropical waters from the cold waters of the Antarctic, which zoom down from 68° to 50° F. Albatrosses appear in the wake of the ship. Between the squalls, gleams of light stream over the shining dark sea, forming white halos standing out against the ocean. There are more and more birds following us, a sign that we are not far from land.

2

This morning at five o'clock, the radar identified the land as de Castries Island. At seven o'clock I catch my first glimpse of the Kerguelen coastline in the mist. A vast land, with monumental cliffs... That doesn't surprise me in the least. I recognized it as my Atlantis in the southern ocean. It looks like no other continent on earth. Perhaps I had seen this unknown landscape in another time, in another life.

You think you are the first. I want to believe that at this very moment I am experiencing the sight, the symbol, the proof, and the feeling that will decide all those to come. I begin to feel uneasy, an impression that grows stronger as the *Marion* approaches the coast. I'll have to identify, organize, and describe this land that seems to rise up out of the primeval chaos; and I have the naïve presumption to believe I'll be able to make it a part of my personal geography.

Yves-Joseph de Kerguelen himself never managed to do that. It was the cause of all his misfortunes. The first sighting of the archipelago was on 12 February 1772. He writes, "At six o'clock in the evening, we sighted a small island four leagues ahead of us."[1] It's a very ordinary sentence, almost bland, and yet the event itself is important. The two ships of the expedition, the *Fortune* and the *Gros-Ventre*, which left Île de France (Mauritius) on 16 January 1772, have just sighted what Kerguelen thinks is a continent. If you make an exception of the explorers of the two poles, Kerguelen, late in the eighteenth century, is one of the last navigators to identify a large landmass. After him the earth is tiny and as light as a Ping-Pong ball. That "small island," in the west of the archipelago, which they named Fortune, is the culmination of a whole lifetime. It could have, and should have, been a sign of glory to come. In point of fact, notoriety brought only suffering, then dishonor, to Kerguelen.

There is an explanation for his total lack of emotion shown at the discovery: Kerguelen wrote about his voyage *after* his troubles. He composed the description without notes and, above all, without his ship's log, taken from him before his trial.

"I publicly presented twenty crowns, as I had promised, to the first sailor to discover land; I promised twice that amount to the first one to see the mainland," Kerguelen notes. However, he doesn't manage to find the island sighted the day before. Finally, at six o'clock the following morning, he is able to write, "I sighted a large, very high headland; for a moment I saw other, equally high land; at seven o'clock, as the sun had dispersed the fog and cleared the horizon, I made out a continuation of land extending as far as the eye could see from the north-east to the south of the compass, comprising twenty-five leagues of coast."

One can't help thinking of the moment when Christopher Columbus first saw America. In the distance he makes out "lights" in the darkness and he thinks they come from land. This land appears, then disappears. Columbus compares it to "a little wax candle rising and falling." This coastline, which suddenly appeared in the moonlight, we now know was an island in the Bahamas Columbus named San Salvador.

If the discoverer of America thought then that he had found Paradise, Kerguelen believed he had just seen Hell. Great disappointment, almost resentment, can be detected in this "continuation of land" he describes. The man who ends the era of great discoveries realizes straight away he has failed. He will never mention that disappointment, but he will always feel bound to his ill-fated island and a victim of the hope he had inspired in his patrons. Kerguelen is like a wretched father presented with the long hoped for heir, whom he realizes is a monster. He won't renounce it. But neither on the first nor the second voyage will he set foot on the new land he has just given to the King of France. Admittedly, the weather was always dreadful. When one day he manages to come very close to land, an inexplicable aversion will make him turn back.

The first man to disembark on the archipelago is the first mate, Lieutenant Charles-Marc de Boisguehenneuc of the *Gros-Ventre*, which is accompanying the *Fortune* with Kerguelen on board. He makes a hasty, almost furtive reconnaissance. In the southern ocean evening, while the men of the *Gros-Ventre* anxiously wait at the entrance to the bay, Boisguehenneuc has a mound of stones made, on which he leaves a bottle containing the text of the claim. "I have displayed the flag and taken possession in the name of my master the King and have ordered three cheers of Long Live the King and the firing of three salvos of musket shot." It is Boisguehenneuc who gives the first description of *"La France australe,"* France in the southern ocean: "The place was covered with mosses, there is wild cress, the terrain is very dark." He thinks he saw "a few trees," which cannot grow in this latitude, any more than the cress.

Everything is oppressive, hurried, and goes wrong during this first landing. A man who Boisguehenneuc has sent up a small hill "to reconnoiter" warns that the *Gros-Ventre* is moving dangerously far away from the coast. A cold drizzle is falling on the bay while the wind is strengthening. As the storm rises, three dull booming sounds are heard. It's the *Gros-Ventre* firing its canon and displaying the blue flag to rally the sailors.

Later, instead of describing what he saw, Kerguelen curiously hands that privilege to a member of Cook's expedition, which explored the archipelago two years after he did, in 1776. Kerguelen takes refuge behind the Englishman's account, as though the truth was too painful for him to describe. In that description quoted by Kerguelen, there is nothing but "storms," "sleet," and "hail." The sea foams with anger and Kerguelen takes a wry pleasure in mentioning that the waves were "as white as milk."

The fiasco of the first voyage contains all the excesses that will characterize the history of the Desolation Islands right up to the middle of the twentieth century. That will be the only name used for that land: Desolation, a place to be left "alone." That name, which was given to it from the first, condemns the Kerguelen archipelago to solitude. It is "desolate," deserted, sad, heartbreaking. Kerguelen seems to say, "*Je suis désolé*" ("I'm sorry"), as if apologizing.

No one realizes that he has miraculously seen what will haunt the imagination at the end of the Enlightenment. It's an incredible thing: no one realizes that this collapsed continent, these surging waters, basalt castles, fields of ruins, and stony silence, which already obsess the poets and feature in paintings, *actually exist.*

Where are the Desolation Islands? Some of the passengers, who know Kerguelen well, are looking at the sea with a somewhat jaundiced eye, not appreciating being so flagrantly contradicted by the mild weather we are having. The coast now has a golden glow growing rosier as the sun rises. These great disintegrating rocks rise up in domes amid a jumble of pebbles, with a sheer drop down to the sea. The pink becomes redder, harder, solider, but also more disturbing. The *Marion* is moving forward slowly and gently, almost gliding. We are in the Morbihan Gulf, much calmer than its Breton counterpart. As the giant seaweed comes in contact with the ship it lazily unfolds until it comes to life in the waters of the wake, like laurel wreaths untied.

The wind has fallen during the night. The now tranquil sea has an almost unbroken surface. Currents run through it, making soft loops in the water like the bends in a stream. It gleams gently like silk being slowly torn by the *Marion*'s stem.

The "poor sailor" leaning over the front of the ship with me can't contain his enthusiasm, "It's so beautiful! I feel I'll get better here."

3

The buildings of Port aux Français slowly glide into our field of vision, as though the boat were running on rails, unwinding a line of hills gently sloping down towards the sea. Seen at a distance the base doesn't look very prepossessing. You feel that the huts, which house about sixty people, were built at random, with no planning or visual appeal. But this insubstantial suburban village open to the elements is still a piece of France. It is so far from everything and so puny looking in that bizarre natural setting. Nature here has a "retarded" look, in the same way as we say someone is "simple."

In a few moments the *Marion* will drop anchor. I don't much like this time just before arrival.

Now I can see the Port aux Français storehouses. With its antennae, pylons, sheds, and dilapidated structures, the base looks like an untidy country barracks or an unfinished industrial zone. A helicopter is hovering around the boat, which is beginning to let out its anchor.

The chains give off a thick cloud of rust as they unwind. The marine anchor holds a special fascination for me: it's like a primitive deity suddenly emerging from a subterranean world. Locked in the bowels of the ship, it's taken out, on show for just a moment, then thrown into the darkness of the deep. No anchor is the same as any other; each one is alive. Sailors say that an anchor has two arms, palms, and a shank.[2]

The *Marion*'s anchor weighs four tons. It's like a night bird beating its wings, frightened at being hauled across the deck. Anchors plunge into the sea like men. The *Marion*'s hesitates, rocks on the surface of the water then boldly dives in. Just as it is about to disappear, the water slows it down and horizontally curbs its descent.

"There's the *disquaire* (record dealer)!" cries one of my fellow passengers.

A man gets out of the helicopter, which has just landed on the *Marion*'s landing deck. A record dealer in Kerguelen! But there are no shops at Port aux Français. I was told the base has a small transmitter that broadcasts rock and French songs. No doubt they meant a *disc jockey*.... He looks energetic but speaks laconically, like a man used to communicating through a walkie-talkie, which he happens to be gripping in his hand as though he means business. This device has become the scepter of the practical man. Give it to the most easygoing person, and he immediately thinks he has to bellow and swagger. Nevertheless the *disquaire* of the Kerguelens looks like a decent guy. I even get the impression he doesn't find the toy very amusing anymore. He says "hello" in a patient, weary voice. It would seem he's an important person at Port aux Français.

We get into a launch. It makes its way with ease through the vast weed beds along the shores of Port aux Français. Sometimes the engine slips. I have an impression of luxuriant marine life in contrast with the bare coastline. I keep saying to myself, "I'm in Kerguelen."

So this is Kerguelen: these barracks, this primeval emptiness, the dullness of the terrain, the slow sad ruin of a world that gives the impression of never having recovered from the original upheaval, the thick stew of seaweed where rocks seem to float! I'm in *"La France australe"* ("France in the southern ocean"), at Port aux Français, on the same latitude as Paris. Does France in the southern ocean really exist?

I put my foot on the concrete jetty. Always this obsession with "the first time." I believe, not without a certain simplicity of mind, that beginnings will reveal a hidden truth. But here, nothing appears. In front of me is the port "office": a joke of a harbor master's office, and empty at that. Just like the countryside. It looks like one of those desolate bus shelters in the French countryside. You never see anyone in them.

There is another thing that's typical of France: giving a name to the smallest alley. A plaque on the road leading to the jetty informs you that you are in the "rue de Boisguehenneuc." This pays homage to the officer of the *Gros-Ventre* who officially took possession of the Kerguelens, an act that shows a touching desire to bring this vast empty space to life by giving it a memory.

The port office is empty, but not the jetty where a welcoming committee is watching for the arrival of the newcomers. This happy band is made up of VATs (Volunteer Technical Assistants), young men who have chosen to do their military service in the Kerguelens. There are about thirty of them, posted to technical services (plumbing, carpentry) or scientific services (marine biology, ornithology, meteorology).

Kerguelen is already making fun of me. What should I do when I first arrive, in the first few minutes? Go through an arch more than six feet high. It's a guard of honor made by the VATs' raised arms. Their faces are painted and they are dressed up like Neptune, naked from the waist up. A plant something like a cloverleaf is offered to the applicant as a sign of welcome. The ceremony is something between "the pleasures of the Enchanted Isle" and an initiation of new students at the École des Beaux-Arts. The tone is both cheeky and slightly embarrassed. The participants are well aware of the element of parody in this arrival. Several of them slip away by jumping off the jetty into the sea. It's February, which is generally the warmest month of the year, and the thermometer has probably reached 59° F, but the sea water is cold. A diver quickly comes to the surface again. "Seven degrees!" Nevertheless, the warmth of the sun and the clear air emphasizing the aridity of the landscape makes a swim seem inviting.

I ponder these first moments on Desolation Island: the curtain rising on a scene like this in the "howling fifties" is something of a hoax. Where then is "the land of eternal storms" described by every traveler who has been here? The archipelago doesn't deserve its sinister reputation. It even seems to have a resemblance to a Breton island of which I'm very fond, called Hoëdic, off Belle-Île. It has the same severity, the same deserted look, the same absence of weathering. Yet there is also something hard and still about it that is rather disturbing.

Besides, there are these imitation natives pulling faces and miming scenes from another world. Are they performing a *ridondaine*, the name the sailors from Brest give to the southern lands because of the contortions that have to be done to reach them?

Suddenly the party is over. The participants, no longer actors in the pantomime, are going up to the barracks again. The passengers who disembarked with me have all disappeared. Port aux Français is deserted. The wind has risen in just a few minutes. It sings in a way I've never heard anywhere else: the voice seems to cover a scale of sounds on one syllable, as if practicing for the difficulties of the major piece to come. The light is fading. Something huge is rising up in front of me.

4

While I'm sitting there on the quay watching the storm building up, a man approaches me. He's wearing a Basque beret that looks rather like a pancake.

"Who are you waiting for?"

"I'd like to know where I'll be staying."

"That's Kerguelen for you," he said, pretending to sound judgmental. "There's no one waiting for you when you arrive and when you go, you'll leave without trace. That's probably why people come here; you can't just blend into the landscape. But enough of that. Let's find your accommodation. I heard you've been given a room in Building L8."

He makes a gesture in the vague direction of a construction just the same as all the others. While we are making our way towards "the village," a familiar cry disturbs the rising scale of the wind, as though its noble song was being mocked by raucous jeers. It's the cry of the seagulls.

They protest loudly, just as they do in Brittany. It's hard to know what dominates, joy or pain. For me, that cry always evokes the tang of the tide. It smells of salt cod bait and bare beaches, where the seagulls love to forage around in the wounds left by the sea as the tide goes out. It also has a whiff of animal piss about it. The nose can easily distinguish these subtleties.

The smell of Kerguelen is a strange one. The cleanness of the wind is deceptive here: elsewhere it usually makes the air seems odorless, but Kerguelen has a lively, fresh smell, as though it came from the depths of the earth.

Seeing me sniffing the air with such concentration, the man

in the beret makes the comment, "The wind is the only enemy in the Kerguelens, because it's unpredictable."

Dark shapes are stirring in a mud pool a few yards away. Sea elephants. They grunt rather menacingly as they wake up, then move from one spot to another with a series of hops. These monstrous animals with their gentle, weepy eyes and drooping mustaches have a look that is expressive, but somehow unfinished. Their trunks are nothing more than nasal deformities; the limbs have not developed beyond flippers; they are as ugly as Quasimodo, yet you can read signs of anger, pain, or bliss, as in humans.

One lands on the pavement. This must be a frequent occurrence as is indicated by a rather comic road sign with a sea elephant on it. The animal's clumsiness is a grotesque parody of the graceful deer seen on signs near forests. This wasteland at the end of the earth displays familiar signs that recall the mother country.

Rabbits run in all directions around the group of huts.

"They're quite tame," my companion explains to me. "They were introduced in 1874 by an English mission. I think they've work out that hunting wasn't permitted around the base. The Kerguelen rabbits are a scourge. As they are in Australia. The burrows increase soil erosion. They destroyed the famous Kerguelen cabbage. This very rare cruciferous plant, a relic of very ancient times, can now only be found on the islands that don't have rabbits."

The ground is covered by a sparse yellow grass, but the most surprising sight is the stones. Dark and shiny like black nuggets, they reveal the volcanic nature of the archipelago.

But there's not one tree. It's above all this absence of trees that gives the impression of emptiness that nothing seems to fill. It destabilizes the site. In France, a line of poplars at the edge of a large property, a single oak in the middle of a field, plane trees along each side of a road separate the parts of the countryside that are open from those that are not, allowing the eye to always get its bearings. Down here, there is nothing to hold your gaze. It's a place without depth, without dominant lines, a blank page on which you can't write anything. In the end, your mind goes dull at always seeing the sea then the mountains wherever you may be on the island. It's like a countdown stuck indefinitely on two figures for fear of reaching zero.

The men have erected a forest of radio antennae and masts like a huge spider web, a kind of net to capture extraterrestrials. A human plea to nature, which could smash this fragile link with civilization with one puff, I imagine.

I go into a building that looks like the temporary classrooms erected as schools at the beginning of the seventies. It houses the crews of two helicopters, who stay in Kerguelen during the summer (November to April).

The man in the beret disappears saying, "We'll be seeing each other." Pictures of naked women line the walls in the passage. There's a little bar knocked together out of pallets, a refrigerator in a corner, and an electric coffeemaker—the whole thing designed to give the illusion of life back in France.

My room comprises a wardrobe, a Formica table, a chair, and a bed. I glance out of my window at this farthest outpost in the world, looking as though it was hastily thrown together by the last survivors of the human race. I now understand what the man in the beret meant when he said, "There's only one thing you want when you're at Port aux Français, and that's to get out of it. But you can't help feeling just a little fondness for it when you come back from a *manip*. Sure it's ugly and boring, but it's the only sign of humanity for a thousand miles around."

What is a *manip*? I suppose it's a *manipulation* (experiment), a scientific operation in the archipelago. Why did he say "a thousand miles around"? I start doing a few calculations. The total area of the Kerguelen Islands is 2,785 square miles, a little larger than the Department of Finistère in France. The archipelago extends from north to south over more than 125 miles and the main island, where I am now, is 88 miles at it largest point. He is probably referring to the position of Kerguelen in the Indian Ocean. The nearest continent is Australia, 3,000 miles away. The closest land is Heard Island, 310 miles to the southeast, but it is even more desolate than Kerguelen, which is not part of the Antarctic world.

How should these islands be classified? Since I arrived, I've noticed that it's difficult to describe and even to conceive of Kerguelen. Every traveler has felt at a loss like this.

When he returns to France, Kerguelen is received at Versailles by Louis XV (18 July 1772). The monarch asks him several questions. He is intrigued by Kerguelen's description of his discovery. "His Majesty asked me if I thought that the lands I had discovered were inhabited. I had the honor to reply to him that the harshness of the climate and the lack of timidity in the birds did not allow that supposition." Kerguelen adds: "His Majesty seemed satisfied with the way in which I had carried out my mission." And indeed, the king announces to him that he is making him a captain and awarding him the Order of Saint Louis.

He is jumping twenty-six lieutenants in the list of seniority, a promotion that will fill a number of people with envy. How can the rumors be stopped? The worst one concerns the *Gros-Ventre*, which at that time has not been accounted for. Kerguelen is accused of having abandoned her. He reports other slanderous claims. "[They say] that I had seen no land, but only a cloud, and that I had ordered the whole crew to keep silent on pain of their lives."

It is certain that Kerguelen's account seemed nebulous enough to Louis XV for the king to command him to organize a second expedition to "verify" his discovery.

The hero of the day lets himself fall into the trap of the enthusiasm his discovery has inspired in the salons. They dictate to him what he has seen. Kerguelen dares not refute it and in the end convinces himself of his illusions. He has seen the Hesperides. He calls the new continent "the third world." Little by little he persuades himself that the desolate land is inhabited by "natives, living in their primitive state, showing neither mistrust nor remorse, and ignorant of the artfulness of civilized men." He even found a word for this new world: *Australasia.* "Monsieur de Maupertuis says that he would prefer to have an hour's conversation with an inhabitant of Australasia than with the finest mind of Europe."[3]

Several indications, both in the preparations for the voyage and the way it was carried out, suggest that Kerguelen had no wish to set out again.

On his return from the second voyage, an order for his arrest is issued and he is put in prison. Kerguelen is accused in particular of "having illicitly taken a girl on board and having lived with her and other female passengers in a scandalous manner." Until they reached Mauritius, three other women besides the unknown beauty had shared Kerguelen's cabin. The clandestine passenger was called Louise Seguin. This storybook character, the mysterious Louison, has often overshadowed the rest. For there really is a "Kerguelen enigma" that has grown up around him and his discovery.

The Kerguelen Islands are strangely like him. There is a struggle between darkness and light; there is natural solitude but also a trace of suffering. I see at least one sign of it: the storm. Kerguelen atones in the wind.

To think that I've made such a long voyage to find myself in this room furnished with a wardrobe and a floral bedcover! I suddenly feel stupid: I've been robbed. It's the corruption of a dream, a confidence trick. Would Port aux Français take away all the illusions I've had about the southern ocean? But is Port aux Français really a part of Kerguelen? From my window I can see the snowy peaks of a mountain.

On the far horizon, distant shapes of rivers, lakes, islands, and winding strips of land are slowly forming. An Arcadian landscape. In the foreground, like a Poussin painting, you can see a pyramid, the capital on a column, gently rounded hills, the huge shadow of ruined towers, with that lapis-lazuli blue that cuts out shapes so sharply that the landscape seems mutilated by it.

5

The day finally came to leave Port aux Français. I went on board the *Aventure* with a few men from the base, heading for the Arch at Christmas Harbor. The *Aventure* is a sixty-foot supply boat that plies the Morbihan Gulf, transporting the people on the winter mission as well as equipment and stores. Like its French namesake, the Morbihan Gulf has its Port Navalo—an anchorage near Royal Channel. Who but a Breton could have named this interior sea dotted with islands and islets? I've brought a thick book with me that I never tire of leafing through: *The Toponomy of the Southern Lands*, which gives the origins of all the place names in the archipelago.

It was Raymond Rallier du Baty, an explorer and navigator from Lorient who, in 1908, gave that name to the very indented gulf that extends far into the interior of the islands. The fact that the ocean goes deep into the heart of the Kerguelen makes exploration easier. Whatever the *Aventure* can do on the water is that much more than can be done on land, which is not easy to travel across.

The sky is dark. The sea has taken on the pale grey color of the petrels that dive into the water as we approach, using their wings to swim. When we pass between two islands, the boat's engine produces a short, sharp sound like a dog lapping. The *Aventure*'s wake leaves traces of a winding canal on the water. The boat goes deep into the fjords, heading straight for the waves and reefs, charging them like a bull, then swerving gracefully at the last minute.

Why does one have this impression that there is something

odd about the place? The green landscapes I'm seeing for the first time could almost be familiar; but there is something missing. Could it be the fluctuating light? Rather than making outlines look hazy, it makes them stand out. The basalt peaks 650 to nearly 1,000 feet high have the hardness and color of bronze, lit up now and then by drops of light. There is a colorless atmosphere around these somber valleys and giant colonnades in spite of all their dull golden lights. What fall sent this Atlantis and its aerial palaces tumbling into the sea? Water has filled the deepest valleys, transforming high mountain chains into islands or peninsulas.

In the middle of the morning we land at a deserted island, leaving two VATs who have the job of tagging sheep. Their stores are packed in barrels with screw-top lids. The point where the *Aventure* came ashore is called Port Bizet on Long Island. The only building on this so-called port is a cabin where the two men will live. They are wearing army parkas and gum boots. Apart from the *Aventure* and the helicopter in the good weather, walking is the only means of exploring the Kerguelens. It's impossible to use normal boots as they sink straight into the soil, which is wet and nearly always spongy.

Port Bizet gets its name from a breed of sheep, introduced on to Long Island in 1958, the *biz̧et* from the Cantal. Ten or so of them are trotting about halfway up the hillside. Others are wallowing in the lush grass. Their wool is so thick and shaggy that at a distance they look like prehistoric animals. This flock of white aurochs gamboling in this unknown savanna accentuates the extraordinarily soft color of the grass. I've never seen such a shade of green, bordering on emerald. The grass is twisted into bundles. One of the passengers, who is leaning, like me, over the front of the boat, and who has been silent until now, notices my surprise. He explains to me that these pastures were sown about twenty years ago.

"Fodder species were introduced to feed the sheep," he said. "We wouldn't do that today. These introduced plants have modified the composition of the original vegetation systems."

His vocabulary is that of a scientist, a language that may have increased our knowledge of the world, but I sometimes wonder whether it hasn't also taken away its charm. My companion explains that by knowingly or unknowingly importing animals such as the sheep, the reindeer, or the bluebottle, and plants like the cocksfoot, man has upset the ecosystem unique to the Kerguelens because of its extreme isolation.

The *ecosystem*! What an ugly word! I must admit I'm allergic to systems, especially if they are linked to the living world. Since nature produced ecosystems (1969), I no longer read La Fontaine's *Fables* with the same pleasure. The concept of the biotope has really taken the poetry out of nature, populated until then with grasshoppers, rabbits, and frogs.

The scientist interrupts my reverie.

"The *biʒet* sheep is a case in point: how has it managed to survive? The climatic conditions are terrible. They gave up shearing the flock and culling some of the lambs a few years ago. The sheep were pretty much left to themselves. But instead of declining, they managed so well that they now show a remarkable resistance, while it's the original stock in France that is declining."

The boat is carefully making its way along the coast of

Long Island, which is more than six miles long. A fence divides one of the hillsides.

"In certain parts of the island, the sheep have eaten everything to the ground," he continues. "The sheep are changed from one enclosed area to the other to build up the pasture again. It's difficult to estimate the number of head: it's in an exponential growth phase and they're talking now of a flock of 4,500. Two to three hundred are slaughtered a year to supply the base with fresh meat. The slaughter of a sheep is like a rite. It's the symbol of a heroic past. The freezers are full of meat."

"A success story like that is rather ironic," I say to him. "I've heard about those two ship owners from Le Havre, the Bossière brothers, who tried to introduce sheep raising into the Kerguelens at the beginning of the century, following the example of the Falklands. Why did they fail?"

"Most likely the choice of site. If you ever get to Port Couvreur, you'll understand all about it. It's a very strange place. There are lots of stories about Port Couvreur. Families of shepherds were still living there at the beginning of the thirties."

The person I'm speaking to is also wearing a military combat uniform. He has the same rather negative attitude as the man in the beret I met when I arrived. What does he do? Where does he come from? He avoids any personal questions. "I take samples." I gather it's his third or fourth stay in the Kerguelens. "In the summer tour of duty," he adds. The summer tour of duty takes place between two visits of the *Marion*, usually from December to April, in the fine weather.

The *Aventure* has picked up speed, skimming past the cliffs as it slips along the narrow waterway between two islands. In the uncertain daylight through a gap in the cliff, I can make out a ruined fortress in the distance, with a cloud of birds wheeling around it. The heavy tower has crumbled at its base, but the walls are still standing.

The boat draws nearer and the dead castle is still there. This fortress was not built from man's labor, but from the whims of nature weathering the basalt. The columns of volcanic rock have formed turrets, spires, and watchtowers. The cliffs falling sheer to the sea look like walls between bastions. The line of fortifications slants as though out of perspective. The incline of the piles of stone and the angle of the walls distorted by the rays of light bursting from the clouds are suddenly illuminated, tortured and grandiose, an arch of light spanning dark ravines.

"Castle Island," the scientist announces.

Shapes moving at the foot of the stone citadel scamper off as the boat approaches. They are old goats peacefully living out their days on the little island. Our arrival has frightened them. They used to be on Long Island and the sound of the boat's engine means they'll be hunted down and taken to Port aux Français.

It's my turn to be dropped off near a cabin. There are some biologists waiting for me before going to Travers Valley to carry out experiments on a *manip*. Then I should get to Irish Bay, close to where *La Curieuse* will be waiting for me. This oceanographic ship is going to Christmas Harbor where the mysterious Kerguelen Arch is situated.

The shape of the landscape is hilly and unexpected; maps

are often unreliable. Some lakes we are going to locate had not been discovered by man even thirty years ago. Travers Valley, which was unknown for a long time, has hot springs only discovered in 1978.

Kerguelen has the privilege of being one of the last places on the planet that has not been thoroughly explored. Nevertheless, everything is more or less known and identified. In fact the unusual thing about the archipelago resides in this "more or less." Desolation Island has been the object of learned studies on magnetism, seismology, cosmic radiation, glaciology, animal biology, etc. But there is no overview. Everything has been identified and yet Kerguelen is still mysterious. I read numerous reports before I left France, but there are always parts that remain obscure. Their research is rigorous but incomplete. They make me think of the Tower of Babel: each one speaks the language of its own discipline and knows nothing of its neighbor's.

Three men come up to meet me. They are VATs who belong to the Laboratory of Marine Biology. One of them is taking samples of insects in Travers Valley. It seems a lot of this work is done on the archipelago.

"Science first gets samples, then observes and finally interprets... when it has time," is the wry comment of the tallest, called Georges.

"Science in the Kerguelens is a pretext for seeing the country," adds the second, who is wearing a military parka. The third is filming our meeting with a video camera.

This self-deprecation is obviously a way of creating good humor and familiarity in our group. The organization of my backpack causes them some amusement. I'd just packed anything I hadn't managed to put into my luggage in badly wrapped parcels, and stacked them one on top of the other. Since my days with the scouts in the fifties, I've had hardly any experience of nomadic life, apart from roaming around a bit in the seventies, like all the men of my generation.

It's three o'clock in the afternoon. With my mountaineer's cap and anorak, plus a pack including Gracie Delépine's *Toponomy*, Rallier du Baty's *Adventures in the Kerguelens,* and Edgar Aubert de la Rüe's *Two Years in the Desolation Islands*, I'm setting off to explore the central plateau and to get to know the land that should lead me to the Arch of Kerguelen. The weather is clear and cool; the light gives the air a saffron tinge, which reminds me of October in Sauternes. There's no shimmer in the light its rays cast on the hillocks, peaks, or valleys. The rock doesn't come to life, although it has all the gradations of black and grey.

The first hours of the trip are tough. I have to get halfway to the top of the rocky ridges overhanging Lake Armor. The water is so pure and deep that the sun can't make it glow. Its brightness is lost in the dim slate grey depths.

Wearing gum boots makes the climb up and then the descent into the dry ravine difficult. I have to put on a good show in front of my young companions, who chat away as they almost absentmindedly step across rocks and streams.

My three companions whistle like canaries, throw stones, and now and again ask me, "Are you okay?" I reply, "Yes," in a toneless voice.

To my relief I can see what looks like a sandy plain, no doubt a dried up pond. We sink into this bog halfway up our calves, but with some delight, even exaggerating the suction of the rubber in the mud. In the distance, the sun is disappearing behind the hills.

Darkness falls very suddenly, knocking down each peak like the ball hitting skittles. The mountains instantly go dark. The light seems to be controlled from some electronic board. We have to hurry to reach the Bossière cabin to the north of the lake of the same name, where we'll spend the night.

We scramble down a waterfall full of pebbles. As I bend down to drink the running water bubbling up through the stones, the weight of my pack makes me fall backwards. There I am looking foolish, flat on my back and stuck between two rocks. The VAT in the parka helps me to my feet. I'm soaking wet. Water is squelching in my boots, but there's no possibility of taking them off as night is falling.

Then we suddenly see the Henry Bossière fjord up ahead of us, ringed with impressive mountains—a Cyclops landscape. The man with the camera is stunned, then begins filming feverishly. A rumbling sound rises, which I can't immediately identify. It's low, like a moan from the kingdom of darkness. I've recognized the deep voice with its endless lament. Blowing on a mountain pierced with holes like a Pan flute, the Kerguelen wind is improvising a tune in the southern night. Orpheus' song eases the violence and the void of the Underworld.

The VAT with the camcorder films the huge shore strewn with thousands of mussels, where the debris of what looks at a distance like a boat is lying on the sand. The ribs of the keel are in fact those of the skeleton of a finback whale. Finbacks are frequent visitors to the Morbihan Gulf, like the famous right whale up in the northern part. For a long while, finbacks could not be hunted because they were much too swift and had the drawback of sinking when they were killed. It was a Norwegian, Svend Foyn, the inventor of the harpoon gun, who had the idea of blowing compressed air into the whale's belly.

How and why did this finback come to die on the banks of this deserted bay? Nothing there now recalls the known world, apart from the huge bank of mussels. Suddenly everything grows dark. The line of the mountains has sunk, as though swallowed up by the waters of the fjord. We grope our way along the shore, guided by the shimmering of the little waves.

The cabin is situated close to a cataract. It suddenly appears in the night, lit by the pale gleam of the foam. But before reaching our shelter, we have to cross the surging waters that crash on to the rocks in big milky bubbles. As in a game of hopscotch, we jump from one stone to the next to reach the last square. And that is the most difficult one. The Bossière cabin is a prefabricated metal shed on piles. It was brought in by helicopter about twenty years ago.

The refuge consists of four bunk beds, a table, and three stools. Most of the provisions are past their expiration date: the canned food bears dates from the seventies. The rest has been eaten by the mice. We go and gather mussels in the icy water for our evening meal. They are as enormous as Spanish mussels. On the sand, we pull them off in whole clumps. After having a thick, hot soup—the mice left a few sachets—I'm too tired to wait for the rest. The mussels are taking an age to cook on one of the tiny portable stoves we have. Although my mattress has several traces of mildew and mouse droppings, I fall blissfully asleep.

The noise of the waterfall is occasionally increased by dull booming sounds, which sometimes wake me. I dream about a mill wheel that has come away from its axle and tumbles down the cascade, shaking the rocks as it falls.

The shock wave travels endlessly through my mind as I sleep.

6

The attractive features of our world are absent from the Bossière fjord. There are no birds. There is no vista in the landscape. The same volume of air links the closest foreground to the farthest background.

What did Henry Bossière intend to do here? What was he looking for in this inlet originally formed by a glacier? Probably nothing at all. He was a governor without subjects, a viceroy of the storm, and it was for his own pleasure that he explored the Kerguelens, conceded to him by the French State in 1893 for fifty years. But when he came here for the first time in 1908, he had another purpose besides looking at his new kingdom. The son of an important shipowner from Le Havre, who was the last Frenchman to fit out a sailing-ship whaler, the *Gustave*, Henry Bossière with his brother René was pursuing a wild dream: to raise sheep on Kerguelen and start up a whaling and sealing industry.

We swallow down a mug of hot coffee. I tell my young friends that before leaving for Kerguelen, I took part in a ceremony honoring the Bossière brothers in Touffreville-la-Corbeline, a village in Normandy.

The two brothers died in the same year, 1941, bankrupt and forgotten by all. Disappointment had not kept them united: before they died they had not seen each other for a long time.

While under the guise of bringing the brothers together in the same grave, this event was intended to restore their memory, tarnished by a scandal in 1931. And yet the brothers were honest. Henry Bossière had obtained the concession of the Kerguelens from the French government. His brother René had received the same rights for other French islands in the southern ocean, Saint Paul and Amsterdam, 1,250 miles northeast of the Kerguelens.

In 1929 René Bossière decided to set up a fishery and small factory on the island of Saint Paul, which had a plentiful lobster supply. The factory closed its door at the end of the season. The foreman asked for volunteers to guard the plant. Seven Bretons offered to stay on Saint Paul. The boat left for France... and the Bretons were forgotten.

In the meantime, the banks had taken over the business. René Bossière wanted to send a boat to bring the employees back, but he was no longer in charge. When "the forgotten men of Saint Paul" were finally picked up, only three remained.... A press campaign was unleashed in France. Public opinion was indignant, ruining the Bossière brothers' dreams for their islands in the southern ocean. Ruined and dishonored, they spend the rest of their lives sad and lonely men. René retired to Touffreville and Henry to Mortagne-au-Perche.

Just as Yves-Joseph de Kerguelen had been tried and defamed for having discovered the Desolation Islands, the two brothers were punished for having restored the lost archipelago to France. Without their vigilance, France would have lost these islands, which had become "ownerless lands." Thanks to them, these rights were asserted and recognized. The Bossière brothers allowed France to be third in the world for "the exclusive economic zone."

After Kerguelen's discovery of the islands in 1772, France lost interest, and the islands were left to whalers, U.S. and English seal hunters, and English, American, and German scientific missions throughout the nineteenth century.

When Henry Bossière was staying in London, he came across a paragraph quite by chance. Australia, which was still a British possession at that time, intended to set up in the Kerguelens. During the Second Empire, an English shipping company had already asked France for permission to establish a coal depot there. The Ministry for the Navy had searched the archives and found Yves-Joseph de Kerguelen's original document claiming possession of the islands. It took interest from the English in these remote isles for the French to realize they belonged to France. No doubt that discovery immediately made them suspicious.

The 1870 war intervened. France forgot "those few damp acres," until Henry Bossière reminded them sixteen years later. Like Kerguelen, the two brothers were victims of an illusion, or rather a fever.

"Could Kerguelen possibly bring bad luck?" asks the man in the parka to whom I've been telling the tragic story of the Bossière brothers. He is twenty-two. He had asked to be sent to Kerguelen.

"Nothing has happened in my life until now!"

7

The dampness absorbs the silence. We left the Bossière cabin for Travers Valley at seven o'clock in fine rain. The lake is the color of pewter. I'm thinking of the curse the man in the parka mentioned with a smile a while ago. Why would the Kerguelens be doomed to misfortune? One day Eden was razed to the ground and thrown into the sea. The oldest oceanic islands in the world are marked by the fall.

Complete silence. Even the stones seem devoid of solid mineral matter. Dante situates his Divine Comedy in the southern hemisphere, under an open sky, in the middle of an impenetrable, empty ocean:

> *Now you have arrived in Purgatory.*
> *See there the cliff that closes it about;*
> *See the entrance there where it seems to part.*

While I was studying the map of the Kerguelens a while ago, I saw that there was a Dante plain and a Dante pass in the south.

We are thirsty from the climb and drink the water caught in hollows in the rocks. It's interesting to see how many bring their hands to their mouths and how many kneel down to drink. The proportions have hardly changed since Gideon in *The Book of Judges*: only one of us scoops up the water in the hollow of his hand.

We are in the world before Genesis. Uninhabited nature, close to original chaos, without landmarks or names. Deadly innocence. Not the least sign of appropriation by man; except for one point. This landscape with its mist fading into the horizon has a name: *val d'Aoste*. The lake below is called Courmayeur, the fast-flowing river, Valdotaine. By asking Adam to name everything in Creation, didn't God give man the power over the animals, plants, and places?

I hate walking. My friends think that I love nature because I have a house in the middle of the Landes forest. They see me as a sort of Francis of Assisi talking to the flowers and the birds. Of course I'm careful not to contradict them. They imagine I wander all alone along the forest paths like Rousseau, while in actual fact I never move from my own home. A whole lifetime is not long enough to explore my own acre.

It's much the same with places as with books. I feel a little sad when I look at my library. What is the use of so many books? I know that at the end of my life, only ten or so books will have been really important. And the others? Glimpses of landscapes very quickly forgotten, passing pleasures. Taking up one thing after another, the fervor, the thrill of the moment, the right to hold opposing opinions, wanderlust: illusions of the seventies. I can see now why I like the Kerguelens. They are the opposite of that fragmentation.

The journey to Christmas Harbor is so long! The Kerguelens are a sort of apprenticeship, and you stay an apprentice for some time. The mortification I feel is only the result of my lack of practice. As I stagger between the stones on the plateau, buffeted by the squall, I realize that I'd lost the habit of walking.

The rain has stopped. There is rocky debris on the ground arranged in perfect geometric shapes. It's so strange and so unexpected that I waste precious time avoiding them for fear of trampling on them. This phenomenon is caused by so much moisture and the continuous alternation between freezing and thaw.

Since we left Bossière, it has been drizzling with rain, just as in Brittany, then the sun shined for an hour—one of those sparkling March suns without much warmth. As the old French proverb goes, it's "affecting but ineffective." When the sun disappeared, the wind came up. I'm quite fond of the Kerguelen wind. It's Ariel, the air sprite, the joker who likes to mystify humans.

The weather has grown cooler. In Kerguelen, the thermometer rarely goes down below minus 41°F. With its very mild summers and winters that aren't too harsh, contrary to its reputation, the climate of Desolation Island is not excessive. They say that it's the land of "the eternal late autumn."

We've been walking for six hours with short breaks now and then. Going up a river, with my boots slipping on the stones covered with tiny algae, seems to take forever. We reach the top of a pass at 1,300 feet high. That may seem a ridiculous altitude, but it's comparable to a height of 9,850 feet in Europe. Points of reference no longer count. You only have to leave the seashore, and in a few minutes you start to feel as though you were 6,500 feet up. The temperature and the vegetation decrease almost instantaneously.

Once we have reached the top, we can see the entrance to Travers Valley, threaded through with dozens of narrow winding rivers like the veins on one of those anatomical illustrations of the body without the skin. The flow of silt-laden water has formed countless deltas. I'm always intrigued by the elasticity of mud. A soft matter rises, soil begins to breathe, working slowly in the layer of mud, in tension with the inert world surrounding it. I've just discovered a mystery; this scene of creation in movement is not meant for me; my looking at it violates its sacred nature. Have I come upon the work of the Creator? "Man shall not see God, and live." (Exodus) I haven't seen God. At the very most I've glimpsed his presence, unless of course it's been an illusion: when you get to the top, you feel a miraculous sense of euphoria that makes up for the fatigue of the climb.

The descent down to Travers Valley is a dangerous one. The stones I lean on can be unstable. They have been perched there above the precipice for 30 million years, the time when the Kerguelens took on the form they have today.

Slabs of rock have fallen down the mountain under the constant action of freezing and thawing, dragging huge avalanches of stones with them. The soil is black with small green tufts here and there, becoming thicker as we go down. It's the acaena (*acaena adscendens*), the commonest plant in the archipelago. I was given a piece as a welcome token when I arrived. This rosaceous plant looks to me something like lucerne. It has the same leaves shaped like butterflies' wings and the same satiny sea green color. It can even be eaten in a salad. Its stalk grows along the ground, sending down roots like strawberry plants, creating new shoots. At this time of the year it has catkins with prickles like those of a thistle, which get into our boots and stick to our socks.

A large expanse of stones at the foot of the mountain slows down our progress. Where does the name Travers Valley come from? Could it be an allusion to the *val de Travers* near Neuchâtel? The orientation of this valley is different from the others, which always go down towards the southeast in parallel patterns.

The emptiness of the Kerguelens would not necessarily appeal to those who like deserts. They are neither dry, nor sterile, nor even arid. Vegetation and life of some kind are rarely absent.

Sometimes the cry of a sooty albatross cuts across the peace of the valley. Nothing is more pitiful than this sad, piercing wail. It's like the entreaty of a human being in the depths of Hell.

Desolation Island is situated in a third region, somewhere between elsewhere and everywhere. Kerguelen didn't know how right he was when he called it *the third world*. It's impossible to see the archipelago on a map of the world in two hemispheres. Not because it's very small—it's actually three times bigger than Réunion, which is marked on most maps—but it's neither one thing nor another, in an in-between area that is just too vast: it's both lost in the ocean between South Africa and Australia and located on the threshold of the Antarctic world, while not actually belonging to it. Could Kerguelen be nothing more than the reality of my life in its pure state? It defies every idea of the picturesque, the exotic, and the voyage. Could I have invented a whole picture of the Desolation Isles before I left France? I carry that kind of devastation within me. All that remains is the purity of the sky and the land, and the awesome newness of creation.

Having been refused a stable geographical home, the Kerguelens are condemned to live in a sort of limbo, a place of penitence, while they wait for a real existence in time and space. They have been sentenced to banishment: they are under French sovereignty, but how many French citizens know that? This denial of existence, however, did not escape everyone. Before I left I found a little work by one René de Semallé, a member of the Société de Géographie. In 1893 he recommended the establishment of a prison colony on Kerguelen, which he presents as "a land of atonement." Semallé praises the advantages of this place of deportation with its "harsh but healthy climate." He adds that "The prisoner condemned to hard labor is compelled to live but not to die."

The project was never taken up, to the great satisfaction of Henry Bossière, who thought that a prison on Kerguelen "would be a great danger to its commercial future." But the idea never really disappeared entirely. In 1979, Michel Aurillac, a member of parliament, proposed the abolition of the death penalty and the establishment of penal transportation to Kerguelen, with a minimum of fifteen years detention in the Desolation Islands. "These islands have the advantage of high security. They are so far from everything that the risk of escape is reduced to zero. Consequently, surveillance there would be relatively easy. The prisoners could engage in agricultural work."

Agricultural work! Apart from the pastures on Long Island and the dandelion, which was illegally introduced, no exogenous plant has ever been able to acclimatize because of the wind. The archipelago does nevertheless possess an abundant flora, some of which are native to the islands, even unique in the world. As I came down the mountain I saw the famous Kerguelen cabbage (*Pringlea antiscorbutica*). This cabbage looks like no other known plant. Perhaps it's a relic from a warmer period. Its growth is very slow and germination can take up to seven months. It's only found now on certain inaccessible mountainsides and on a few islands.

It's too late to reach the Travers Valley cabin. I'm told there is a cave nearby in the side of the mountain, which can serve as a shelter for the night. Having felt our way for an hour, we finally come to a shallow cave. A barrel of provisions has been left there. You only have to unscrew the lid to open it. Great use is made of these plastic barrels for transporting and preserving food on the Kerguelens. A document inside shows that these stores were left in 1984. We find a bag of hazelnuts and to our surprise, they are still edible. They will be part of our evening meal with some canned pâté spread on a slice of "*manip* bread" we have brought with us. This bread is made by the baker at the base. It has a very heavy consistency and the soft, damp interior of the loaf lasts for a long time.

The night is cool. The murmur of flowing water and a dull, rustling sound fill my sleep like an unpleasant buzz.

Strange noises haunt the night. Moans that could be either joy or pain, rattles that sometimes strike melodious notes, clanking, stamping, lapping, sighing, gurgling, sounds endlessly shivering through the gloom. These sounds come from the earth and not from outside. They come in an oppressive ebb and flow like the surf, pushing back the silence in waves.

This subterranean rumination slowly lulls me and I finally fall deeply asleep.

8

The red color of a sleeping bag, various items of clothing at the entrance to the cave, even the sound of our voices are just an insignificant speck on the landscape. We're not out of place here, we don't really exist. We are absent from this apparently limitless world. Lines and mass and color of rock are there for themselves, not for us. Clouds, water, and light, which usually give a sense of security, here suggest nothing at all.

And yet the power of the morning is overwhelming: the water in the streams, the bronze of the basalt rocks, the fields of acaena shining brightly in the sun, and the extraordinary clearness of the air. In the Kerguelens, the intense circulation of the atmosphere sweeps away the moisture, cleaning the air and making it shine like a two-way mirror as soon as the sun comes out. Everything has a sharpness and firmness of outline that expresses the triumph of nature. The dew, essence of the morning, has placed little silver balls in the hollows of the acaena leaves. Like tears of mercury, they roll without joining together.

The weather is fine and walking should be less taxing today. We're in no hurry to strike camp. Propped up between two rocks, I'm reading *Adventures in the Kerguelens* by the navigator Raymond Rallier du Baty.

The author tells us that he has brought the works of Horace with him. He feels the same sense of unreality reading his favorite Latin poet in the landscapes of the Desolation Islands as I do reading his work. I've never read such a strange adventure book. Rallier du Baty also fell in love with the Kerguelens at some stage. He took refuge in them like someone locking himself away in a Carthusian monastery. There's nothing mystical, however, in his move. In the same way as his master Horace, he acknowledges he has discovered the simple country life.

He leaves Cherbourg on 13 October 1907 on a 65-foot sailing ship with a crew of four men under the official command of his brother Henry, but he, Raymond, is the real head of the expedition. He is twenty-six. After a fairly rough passage, he reaches Kerguelen in March 1908. In his account of the voyage, he describes the uneasiness that came over him as he set foot for the first time on the deserted ground of the Desolation Islands. The first thing that struck him was "the heavy silence of the archipelago." He writes: "It is a silence that nothing had broken since the first upheavals of nature in the world's cauldron."

Then he discovers the Arched Rock at Christmas Harbor, which looks like a fortress rising up out of "the kingdom of the dead." He assures us in his description that the arch is nearly 150 feet high, whereas it is really more than twice that height (335 feet). He anchors at the far end of the bay "with high ramparts of black basalt towering over them."

He is surprised to discover birds that look like wood grouse or teal. He fires a shot. It's the first time the sound of a firearm has ever echoed in that place. Rallier du Baty spends some time describing the agitation of the animals coming into contact with humans for the first time. Once again, this obsession with the original act, the first gesture.

All the accounts by travelers describe the trusting relationship of animals with man. Rallier du Baty naturally refers to Robinson Crusoe. One remembers the first time Robinson kills anything. He is surprised how easily he can slaughter wild animals; he feels proud and sickened at the same time. The bird Rallier du Baty kills with the same feeling of shame is none other than a Kerguelen pintail, which is very good to eat. Today it can only be hunted from May to October, outside of the breeding season.

When Rallier du Baty arrived in March 1908, there was not a living soul in the archipelago. With his five companions, he was totally cut off from civilization and had to find food wherever they were to survive, "coming close to Nature in its wildest and most primitive form."

The author tells of a trek in the central plateau through "a series of valleys and fresh-water lakes, in the midst of black and sinister mountains that rose rugged and steep." And he adds, "That made me think of a journey through Dante's Inferno, for the landscapes reminded me of the famous illustrations of the mountains by Gustave Doré. This evocation of damnation does not prevent him from being fascinated by the Desolation Islands. He explains this paradox very well: "Seen through the drizzling rain, its sinister ugliness really gave it a hellish atmosphere, a land of wild, bare desolation, shunned by both angels and mortals. On a fine day with the sunlight sparkling, everything is different. The particular beauty of the Kerguelens creeps into one's heart." Rallier warns the reader that he has given an unadorned account of his adventures, but his descriptions show that he cannot work out the mystery of Kerguelen and is fascinated by that inability.

Unlike Kerguelen, Rallier was not taken in by the Desolations. He made two journeys there. When he realized how dangerously seductive they could be, he never came back. That is why his name and his adventure are still not known. The postscript in his book shows that the French have never acknowledged the worth of Rallier du Baty, who died in 1978 at the age of ninety-seven. The work I'm reading now in the landscape he loved was published in English in 1911. It was prepared with the help of a British journalist, who made a direct translation of his account. A French publisher has just recently decided to publish this testimony.

"The spirit like the wind hovered over the face of the waters," says Genesis. The wind in the Kerguelens is always lying in wait like the skua, the vulture of the Desolations. We have to leave in a hurry. Clouds in the shape of cigars or dirigibles are appearing in the sky. The Kerguelens have this "hellish" atmosphere described by Rallier.

Whirlwinds rising deep in the valley release clouds of ochre dust. We leave as fast as we can in the rather vain hope of getting away from the storm, like Orpheus, leaving the realm of Hades behind us and going forward towards the life-giving daylight. We don't turn around, as we are fully occupied struggling against the gale.

The sky ahead of us is torn in half, revealing a huge blue rift. We run towards it, hoping for its protection to get us out of trouble, but as we move forward, the bright break in the clouds also moves away.

I discover at last why the Kerguelen wind is unique: it never whistles. There are no obstacles in its path: no trees, no houses, no electric wires, no fences. Instead of filling the air with the sharp notes we are used to in the "civilized" lands, it gives out a muffled roar. Its voice has the depth and power of chanting in the Greek Orthodox liturgy.

A rumbling, thundery sound is growing louder in the valley. The wind shudders like an avalanche. It's coming down; it will catch us.

I feel as though gusts of wind are hitting our backs like falling stones. The ground is vibrating, and I'm frightened: I've never known such a strength of wind.

This valley I thought was dead taught me why the origin of the world is in the wind.

I can not only hear this cosmic whirlwind, I can see it. While I'm hastily looking for shelter behind some rocks, I think I'm seeing the moment when the world began with the storm. Its breath is awesome.... It brings a landscape that seemed to have lost consciousness back to life again.

I fall over twice, almost lifted off my feet by the squall, and am only saved by stumbling into a natural trench in the ground protected by a mound of stones. The movement of a waterfall down the mountainside in front of me seems to have stopped, yet the water isn't still. It looks like a long scarf pinned to the mountain. It doesn't float, but swings like the pendulum of a metronome out of control. Actually, the water isn't falling; it's being pushed up by the force of the wind. Instead of making the water explode into little drops, the storm channels it so that it looks as though it's hanging vertically in the air.

I'm kept a prisoner here in my shelter for several hours. My companions have taken refuge a little further on behind some rocks. We wave to each other from time to time. There are balls twirling about in the gale and I watch them as they whiz past. They are light, perfectly round and about the size of a croquet ball. Looking at the moss on a rock, I realize what this strange phenomenon is. The moss is ripped off by the wind, which makes it roll over and over on itself, giving it that perfectly round shape. These thunder balls bounce off the rocks at incredible speed. I feel almost paralyzed, overwhelmed by nature in such a fury.

Yves-Joseph de Kerguelen himself was a victim of this sluggishness/numbness on his second voyage in 1773. When he is actually there at the Desolation Islands, he is incapable of taking any action. He shows a kind of passive, probably unconscious, resistance to his discovery. The investigation for the trial on his return shows his stubborn determination to repudiate his discovery. The king's commissioners in charge of the inquiry emphasize this fact: "He never managed to find a favorable day to go and anchor in a fine bay the frigate L'Oiseau had discovered and even sounded." One morning he seems to have at last decided to drop anchor in said bay, "but after a quarter of an hour, he rallied the frigate and took a tack to the open sea." The reasons he gives for this are incomprehensible. Kerguelen seems to boycott his discovery. He will always avoid getting off the ship, moving around the archipelago for more than a month before making his escape.

The wind, the isolation, and the nature of the terrain impose moderation. It's important to stop when the wind is blowing, to eat only when you are hungry and to make camp when night falls. This happens when we are making our way towards the Travers Valley cabin. The darkness has suddenly risen up out of the distance, making the outlines of valleys and hills disappear as it approaches.

It's a race against time between the two of us. We walk for an hour along the cutoff of a river rather like the treacherous sandy *rios* of the Loire. I can feel the contact of the cold water on my boots and its rather unpleasant pressure suddenly twisting around the rubber like a snake.

Mists rise up in front of us in the gloom and then suddenly fade away. These mysterious swirls of vapor seem to come from a waterfall. With each step, our boots produce a short, soft, lapping sound.

A dull beat like the sound of a drum reverberates in the air. The mist sometimes rises up and forms a plume with flashes of quicksilver. Its indistinct light comes and goes in the shadows. We make our way towards it with some apprehension, listening to the tom-tom sound growing longer and more flowing. Now it sounds like running water.

We have just come upon the Travers Valley thermal springs. Twenty years ago, no one knew they existed. They flow from a hilltop and tumble down hitting the rocks and forming a stream. The cabin, which is close to the springs, should soon be coming into view, but we still can't find it.

I'm tired of walking. We make our way forward on the wet ground, hardly being able to see where we are going and trying to make out shapes in the dark. The cabin is still nowhere to be seen. Just as we begin to fear we may have to spend the night outdoors, someone ahead lets out a cry of joy.

Near a metal barrel, which serves as a marker, there is the Travers Valley cabin at last, hidden behind a fold in the formation of the land. It's tiny but still fairly comfortable. I unroll my sleeping bag and fall asleep immediately.

At about three o'clock in the morning the wind rises. I can hear it building up with one enormous intake of breath. I wait for the moment it starts breathing out again. It never comes. I sleep lightly, troubled by the breath that is never released.

PART TWO

The Sheet Anchor

"We saw a world of grit and ash."

Alan Sillitoe

I

The wind shakes the cabin and pushes in the corrugated iron that suddenly loses its tension, producing a resounding gong. There's no hope of going outside. Snug and warm in my sleeping bag, I continue reading the adventures of Rallier with my copy of Delépine's *Toponomy* close at hand. I enjoy listening to the storm while reading out loud the passages that refer to our present situation. I inform my companions that Rallier experienced a storm lasting thirty days without a break.

"Shut in for thirty days! That's dreadful."

"What are you complaining about?" I ask them. "We've got food and books."

Georges ventured outside, but when the door closed, it shook the cabin to its foundations.

"At first the wind blew from the north in gusts with a deep, mournful roar as if a huge pack of mad beasts were charging."

Rallier had to face terrible problems. He narrowly escaped death several times, but he never attaches great importance to it. One day he decides to explore the central plateau with one of his sailors, Léon Agnès. He has no shelters or huts like we do and makes do with a tent, which the wind likes to tear down, preferably in the middle of the night. It never stops raining during his expeditions. The two men wake up every morning soaked to the skin with their sleeping bags floating in puddles of icy water.

While they are following the shore of an unknown lake, Rallier du Baty decides to name it Agnès.

The Delépine book notes that the name was not retained later by the five-member Toponymy Commission whose functions are described at the beginning of his "guide." Its task seems absurd. Why give rulings about the names of uninhabited islands? The Commission, which met in Paris between 1966 and 1971, undertakes to grant that the Kerguelen Islands officially exist. The head of department for the French Southern and Antarctic Territories (TAAF), who rules over our distant areas from Paris, realizes then that just occupying a territory is not sufficient to possess it. Its lakes, rivers, valleys, and gulfs have to be given definite names. As Kerguelen was visited in the nineteenth century mainly by British and American whalers and sealers, there are many English appellations. After 1950 French names were added to these by personnel at the Port aux Français base.

Some order had to be imposed on this chaos. Delépine states that the Commission's rulings gave priority to French names. Names of people still living, given after 1950, were eliminated. In spite of that, the Kerguelens are studded with Josette Lakes, Danièle Valleys, and Isabelle Peninsulas, which would appear to honor the wives of scientists on missions in the Kerguelens.

The Commission declared it had decided not to finish its work. An admirable act of humility, not without a sense of the poetic, and leaving the door still open for the imagination. By respecting the still numerous blanks on the map, they left it to members of future reconnaissance teams to invent place names. The Commission did such a good job turning back time that it ended up transforming it into a space full of "holes." Since the nineteenth century, which saw the Humbolds, the Brazzas, and the Stanleys penetrate deep into the interior of the continents to complete their exploration, the smallest recesses of the world have been given a name. The Kerguelens still escape being completely surveyed and registered like the rest of the world.

Yet the Kerguelens are full of names that give the impression of a game made up by children. They could have been amusing themselves by inventing an ideal island based on their heroes (Mount d'Artagnan, Mts. Porthos, Athos, and Aramis), members of their families (Lake Henri, Lake Christian, Camille Islet, Anita Peak, Lake Nicole, Liliane landmark), and their favorite books (*Wuthering Heights*, the *Château d'If*). There is a Fairy Mountain, a Bathtub Lake, a Pedestal Table Summit. Could the Kerguelens be that allegorical country where every river and mountain has a meaning known only to the person who named it, like the carte du Tendre?[1] There is actually a Christian name, Marie-Rose, hidden in Lake Marioz, with its Savoyard overtones. There is Doubt River, and Setback River recalling the difficulties encountered by an ornithologist on one of his reconnaissance trips. As they are islands without women, the Kerguelens bear the signs of a deprivation that has inspired husbands to celebrate their wives back in France. Not that it stopped them from dreaming about other female figures: Aphrodite, which is a lake, and Venus, obviously a mount. There is also a Navel, which is a rocky out-crop on the Cook Glacier, and a peak called the Big Breast.

And we shouldn't forget the mysterious Louison, who has a cove named after her. Louison, the first woman ever to come to the Desolation Islands.

Kerguelen hid her on board on his second voyage. She shoul-dered responsibility for all the grievances subsequently ascribed to the leader of the expedition. Why did this sailor, usually concerned about rules and regulations, dare to take the girl along. He suspected she would prove disastrous for him. Louison is the Eve of Kerguelen: she brings both sensual pleasure and misfortune. The discoverer of that ravaged Eden is cast out from his discovery before he can even take posses-sion of it. "Because you have heeded the voice of woman, cursed is the ground for your sake." The primal curse still hangs over the archipelago.

Excited by Louison's presence, but disappointed at not being able to approach her—Louison belongs to the captain—the young officers loosed their anger and frustration on Kerguelen. The investigation for the court case mentions that one of them, du Cheryon, "wished to share the favors of that girl, and the other female passengers, with his captain." This leads one to believe that Kerguelen enjoyed the favors of the four passen-gers. The report continues: "This claim, which could only have inspired jealousy of M. de Kerguelen, created rivalry between these two officers for the exclusive possession of the girl, a rivalry most prejudicial to the good of the service by affecting the harmony that should reign in a vessel and weakening the respect due to authority." It's likely that being aware of the bad example he was setting the crew, Kerguelen felt guilty and unsure of his authority. Hence his constant hesitation, his lack of resolution, and, in short, his anxiety on the second voyage. "I can assure you Sir, that I am sick of being in charge of men," he writes on his return.

Kerguelen's offense is not having taken Louison with him and gone against the king's instructions, but of having discovered the Desolations. He feels oppressed because he committed the unforgivable sin: killing hope. In his glory days, he had written: "In short, France in the southern seas will display wonderful examples, both physical and mental." He is conscious of having betrayed the expectations of the king, the court, the philosophers, and scientists, who believed in the real existence of a France in the southern seas. For more than a century, France will maintain its ban on the islands even though they belong to her.

Kerguelen states that he decided to set off back to France because of the number of sick people aboard. But he acts strangely in this also. He draws up a report that he orders his officers to sign. This document mentions 120 to 130 people on the sick list and the stores that have gone bad, especially the biscuit ruined by sea water coming in from above. Why did the food deteriorate so quickly? Because Kerguelen was not vigilant enough. During the preparations for the second voyage he is inattentive and does not bother to supervise the loading of the ship. One can imagine his obsessive fear of doing the long journey again: he knows from his first voyage that there is nothing to be gained from that land.

I decide to go to the thermal springs not far from the cabin to relieve my fatigue. The waterfall flows into the valley through a stream that goes right through a prairie of acaena. The water has hollowed out several ponds each the size of a big bathtub. In the first, the water is boiling hot; the temperature of the tub halfway down seems more bearable. I quickly take my clothes off and get in. The air really is very cool and there's a drizzle of rain now and again.

I've stretched out on the moss next to my *caldarium* and lie there for nearly an hour, watching the movement of the clouds in the sky, occasionally wiping away some rain that cooled my hot face. The only living creature in this landscape is a skua, which takes a dive at me. Its long grey wings actually brush against me. Wheeling around above the white shape lying on the ground, he then comes down and swoops close to the ground to defy me. Then he lands close to me and approaches cautiously, almost humbly. I'm suspicious of his apparent shyness: the skua is the raptor of the Kerguelens. He attacks birds to steal the young in their nests and kills a lot of baby rabbits he hunts down deep in their burrows. He hops about with his wings spread, pretending to take no interest in me, but his cold, patient, treacherous eyes are trying to work out who I am. He stays with me for a long time, coming closer and closer until I clap my hands to chase him away.

Travers Valley is a restful, disused place, an enclave of noth-ingness, something at a standstill, empty. I'm separated from the rest of the world by a line of crenellated hills—my Wall of China! I must be light-headed after the hot bath: there is some-thing basic and instinctive about this torpor coming over me.

I'm floating on nothing with my face to the firmament. I'm floating on the surface of this upturned bowl of the sky. In its depths, I can make out the red and ochre inlay of the little clouds misshapen by a marbling of veins and spots, but otherwise looking just like a mosaic in a swimming pool, which seems curved when you see it through deep water.

Our evening meal consists of pasta and a bottle of Côtes de Provence we found at the bottom of a barrel. I enjoy its pleasant, unassuming, rustic character. Who would have agreed to weigh down his pack so that he could drink a Côtes de Provence in Travers Valley? We try to imagine the odyssey of this bottle before it ended up so mysteriously in our cabin. It began its life in a vineyard near Aix, set sail in Marseilles, went through the Suez Canal, suffered the heat of the Tropics then the buffeting of the "roaring forties." It was put ashore in Port aux Français then carried by a member of a winter mission to the other end of the archipelago.

There is nothing on the cork but a date: 1985. We each take a turn to hold it, pressing the cork, running a finger gently over the date, as if it could reveal some secret. No one has come to Travers Valley for months. In Kerguelen, it's as though what took place last year never happened. One mission leaves; another takes its place. Each one knows nothing about the one before. The Kerguelians have no memory. "That which has been is what will be, that which is done is what will be done." No events or stories are passed on to the next mission. There is a lack of illusion in this succession of temporary colonies that recalls Ecclesiastes. Perhaps it's because of the wind. "I have seen all the works that are done under the sun; and indeed, all is vanity and grasping for the wind."

Although France officially has authority over this territory, it's actually the wind that controls the archipelago. That is the reason why France delayed so long in exercising its sovereignty over Kerguelen. Up against the wind, there is no chance of dominating anything. Burning deserts, icy wastes, or wet climates can be brought under control. Not the wind. "No man has power over the wind to imprison the wind," to quote Ecclesiastes once again. The wind in the Kerguelens proclaims the absolute fluidity of things. The present moment has no depth; what is to come has no future. This instability and the feeling that time has no substance have not escaped my companions. Knowing that nothing will remain after we leave, they are inclined to live in the present and care little about what has just happened. They feel no doubt or regret. That may be because they are young. I really like them, these three new friends of mine. Unfailingly good humored, carefree, but sensible when faced with even a minor obstacle, they treat this "third world" with a kind of deference.

I come across a book someone left behind in the corner of the cabin. It's Pierre Mac Orlan's *Sheet Anchor*. I read it when I was a kid in the same exotic gleaming "Red and Gold" Collection, which for me had the saffron glow of the Society Islands. This forgotten book made me think of the family bake house where I used to read sitting on a half-full flour sack. I would push it into shape like one of those seats filled with kapok, so that I could lean my back against it. Adventure blew at force seven or eight in the oven and the heat was tropical.

After having read it right through during the night by flashlight, I feel so puzzled I can't go to sleep. In the first place, someone has written annotations in the book. But the passages underlined make no sense. The ones that have been picked out are not the most striking, nor are they the most effective descriptions. They are dialogues, on the face of it quite uninteresting ones. The story takes place in Brest during the decade 1770 to 1780, exactly the period when Kerguelen lived there himself. He began his career in the marine guards. He embarked from there for his second voyage to the southern seas on 26 March 1773. He disembarked there on his return on 7 September 1774. He will also be put in prison and tried in Brest in an old ship used as a hulk anchored in the Penfeld River. Now Mac Orlan's novel takes place precisely in this part of Brest where the hero's father had a shop at the sign of the Sheet Anchor. This is the strongest anchor on the ship.[2] Every time Penfeld is mentioned, my mysterious reader has underlined it. Why?

I believe in fate, not coincidence. It's quite natural for a man spending a year in the Kerguelen Islands to be interested in the man who discovered them. But did he really read this book because of Kerguelen? Perhaps he was a Breton, from Brest? Someone might have told him about *The Sheet Anchor* set in his hometown. He might have brought the book to Kerguelen, without doubt the best place in the world to catch up on one's reading.

I'd forgotten the naval surgeon Burns, the main character in *The Sheet Anchor*. In his opinion adventure is a sham, "a lively amusement for clerks and pampered adolescents." He goes even further: "The occupations that seemed the most likely to accept adventure were the first to reduce it to nothing."

What a shock when the boy I was then began to suspect that the honorable Dr. Burns was really a pirate whose cruelty and daring terrorized the good people! Yet Burns was so gentle, so indulgent, so philosophical. In the end, when he was unmasked, he was hanged and I suffered nearly as much as the hero of the novel himself. How could two such different beings coexist in the same person? *The Sheet Anchor* should have destroyed my childhood innocence, but I don't remember having appreciated the attraction of ambiguity then, nor even having understood the disturbing game of hide-and-seek that was going on right up to the final revelation. I didn't know that this rather painful and inexplicable entertainment was called literature.

We leave at dawn for Irish Bay, where the *Curieuse* should pick me up late in the afternoon. I decide to accompany my friends to Bellows Pass (*col de la Soufflerie*). The stream we are following winds its way through fallen earth and rock. On the heights bathed in a light I now know well, a rather cool aggressive wind is blowing. That light has the brightness of April days in France when the sun and rain engage in one skirmish after another. It's impossible to know which one will win: when the sky is clear of showers, it seems so clear that you can hardly explain how it can become so dark just a few minutes later. From Bellows Pass you can see the whole of the Valley of Wonders (*la vallée des Merveilles*). A wealth of unknown landscapes opens up before us: deserts, lakes, hills, and rivers. A mysterious ripple of mist moves over them, making the air with its swirls of warm currents seem to quiver. The silent plains, the muddy water falling in heavy drops from the glacier, the lonely rivulets, the black, topless towers, the green prairies are all bathed in a cerulean light as though they had been delicately dipped in ash and dried in the sun. If you look at them individually, these landscapes have neither the grey color or the powdery look of ash, but its lightness and bluish hue, which softens and molds every line and shape, gives them a hazy luminosity like the *sfumato* of Leonardo's landscapes.

"And the Lord showed him from there the whole land from Galaad to Dan." I know that I will never reach that land. I must be satisfied with gazing at it longingly. All this for a very mundane reason: it's too far and I'm only a tourist. But I don't want to miss anything; I'm "doing" Kerguelen as others "do" the Cyclades islands or the churches of Cappadoccia. I find this inelegant word appropriate for me. You "do" a country as you execute a work, according to a plan or a timetable. Execute, that's the right word. By telling my story of this country, I know that I'm destroying something of its totality.

We take another route back to Irish Bay. As this valley has never been named nor even marked on the map, we convince ourselves that we are the first to explore it. Water leaps down between the rocks, between the steep walls it has cut through like a saw. Until now we've never seen canyons like it, with steep sides sometimes 325 feet high. The clear water has bored through the rock, opening wide gullies. Sometimes it lingers in basins, just like natural swimming pools, which make you think of the *planiols* in the limestone plateaus of south-central France.

The water is so clear in the summer light that it makes you want to take a dip. The sun and wind have made us red in the face, but we just had to dip our hands in to be pierced by the icy cold.

The prairies of acaena become denser and denser. In the sunlight they give off a rich, heavy smell with an acid edge, green as the taste of grape stalk, difficult to classify. It's something like the smell of new hay and the pungency of ivy in the hot midday sun. The boggy ground cracks and spreads into smooth flat shapes. We sometimes sink into muddy patches hidden by the clumps of acaena, huge sponges saturated with a rusty-colored water giving off a slightly sharp, fermented smell like yeast.

As we come to Lake Bontemps at the end of our expedition, we decide to give a name to this unknown valley. My friends suggest the name Mac Orlan. I point out to them that given the writer's maritime source of inspiration, it would be more appropriate to give his name to a cape or a cove. My friends insist. So Mac Orlan it will be.

What we have just performed is an extremely serious act. Simply by naming this valley, we have taken away its untouched state. My companions want me to submit *Mac Orlan Valley* to the Toponymy Commission. I'll do no such thing. May this valley rest in peace, forgotten by mankind for a long time to come! They will inevitably brand it one day with a name.

Lake Bontemps is not far from our cabin. The calm waters covering about six miles seem to stay even beside the ocean. They are prevented from flowing down into the foaming waves by a thin strip of land protecting the lake. We cross long stretches of shoreline. Flocks of birds fly off as we approach with a sharp, loud beating of wings. This explosion moves suddenly through the air like sails lowered at the same time.

The startled cries cease, leaving a grey stretch of ground as still and mournful as bare reclaimed land. It's the dry sand and endless ridges that suggest the comparison. Surrounded by the remains of several former beaches, there is something indolent, prostrate, even depressed about the shores of this lake. It shows that the sea was once at least three feet above the present height.

Lines of pebbles delicately fitting together form such regularly shaped mosaics on the grey sand that you suspect a human hand has shaped them. Georges assures me, however, that it's a natural phenomenon, but I don't really understand his description. Scientific explanations bore me to death, but I take the easy way out and pretend to follow, trying to look knowledgeable. The lake spills into the sea down a very high waterfall. The water spreads out in bursts. The surface of the lake is calm while just a few yards away the sea is flecked with foam in a series of short, sharp waves. The blinding light highlights the icy roughness of the ocean. But where is the *Curieuse*?

Sitting sheltered in the hollow of a little inlet, I'm watching a group of terns vainly trying to fly against the wind. The tern, which is also called the sea swallow because of its forked tail and pointed wings, is found all along the Kerguelen coast, picking little crustaceans out of the seaweed beds. Surprised by the force of the wind, the birds can't move forward and are sometimes thrown backwards. In the end, one of the terns decides to take an oblique path, but an even stronger gust of wind throws it into the waves. I don't see it come up again.

Large clouds suddenly fill the horizon like billows of smoke. The wind whips up the sea and breaks it into thousands of flecks of foam. The ocean seethes; it steams and smokes like a boiler, an erupting liquid volcano spitting froth everywhere, ash grey geysers. The whip of these wings of foam whirls around like a cloud of frightened birds....

The *Curieuse* won't be coming. I have to come back to Port aux Français and find another way of getting to Christmas Harbor.

Back to the Travers Valley cabin. Mysterious forces seem to prowl in the shadows. The wind gently moves the crockery we left outside, slides around the walls of the cabin and drums on the roof. Once night has fallen, we retreat shivering into our twenty-five-foot hut and open tins of cassoulet or sharp-tasting sauerkraut that make us think of France. We read and reread the writing on the labels mentioning the place of manufacture and the recipe.

In the distance, the rumbling of Lake Bontemps shakes the air like muffled cannon fire. It's the night battle between water and wind. The sailor who gave his name to the lake, Jean Bontemps, is neatly described in Rallier's account: "He was superstitious, stubborn, a man of few words, but phenomenally strong and absolutely loyal to those in command. We asked no more of him than that."

My copy of Delépine mentions that *lac Bontemps* was originally named Fresh Water Lake in 1799 by Captain Robert Rhodes, who was one of the first sealers and whalers to come to Kerguelen. Robert Rhodes made a remarkable survey of the northeast coast. His hand-drawn map, kept in the archives of the British Hydrographic Department, carries a dedication to George III, "under whose authority and gracious patronage a considerable part of the southern hemisphere was explored." Delépine points out that this comment proves French exploration had been forgotten at that time. It also shows how little importance the English and Americans attached to French sovereignty over the Desolation Islands. At that time no one really knew to whom that land belonged. Between its discovery by Kerguelen in 1772 and the ship *L'Eure* taking possession of it again in 1893, only one French ship will land on the archipelago: the *Sally*, under the command of Captain Peron, in 1800.

Eight years earlier, Peron had agreed to stay on Saint Paul Island with four sailors to hunt sea lions. But his ship never returned and he owed his salvation three years later to a passing English ship. Because there was not enough room on the English boat, the hundreds of sea lion skins, which were worth a fortune, could not be taken on board. Peron's story is strangely similar to that of the seven Bretons abandoned on the same island in 1929. It was as though these southern lands were doomed to the same tragic myths from the very beginning: the hope of Eldorado that turns out to be a hell, abandonment and loneliness on an uninhabited island, treasure that can be of no use, like the lode of diamonds discovered by Robinson Crusoe.

I listen to the sound of the rain endlessly streaming down. It muffles the dull boom coming from Lake Bontemps. This is a soft noise. Nothing in common with the loud, gurgling sounds of a downpour as it falls heavily on the branches of trees or the asphalt in towns.

2

Georges is inspecting his samples. His receptacles for catching insects were all around the room. He has shown me how to observe them under stones, in the mosses or the peat bogs. The Kerguelen insects are wingless. They can't fly because of the extremely violent wind, which finally caused their wings to atrophy. Several other insects, however, arrived with man, for example the bluebottle you find now in Port aux Français. It has taken over the territory formerly occupied by the wingless flies, which have taken up residence in rotting soils, roots, and washed-up seaweed. A dozen or so insects are flying about, imprisoned in the tubs set up by Georges.

The black rocks are spotted with tartarous deposits. In the dawn light, the basalt turns dark red. There is a whitish sheen on the surface of these masses of stone, like the patina you find in vineyard buildings where the wine is made. A grape-growing friend once told me that the word *tartar* came from Tartar and that this crust was the sign of devilish alchemy.

Georges suddenly lets out a cry of excitement.

"A bluebottle! Our dear old French fly! No one has ever reported it in this part of the island!"

We are witnessing an important discovery.

"How did this blowfly manage to reach this lost valley? It certainly didn't fly all the way from Port aux Français. So, it must have hidden away in the provisions." Georges adds with a certain solemnity, "Man never arrives anywhere alone. He must always be accompanied by the blowfly and the rat. In that way, we know that a place is civilized."

The sky is slowly becoming overcast. The foehn effects created by the west wind bring strange cloud formations like stiff-shaped zeppelins slowly moving across the sky. They say that there is never a day without rain in Kerguelen, but never a day without sun either. It has been established that the archipelago gets as much sun as Biarritz, the fashionable French beach resort.

Trying to describe the color of the sky has always seemed to me one of the noblest and wisest of man's occupations. We may laugh at meteorologists, but we listen to them and excuse their blunders. I never tire of hearing that "there are no seasons any more." Looking at the sky unites the two principles on which our human condition has always been based: hope and the unexpected. These virtues are active in Kerguelen. The ever-changing sky has the promise of a sunny spell or a gathering storm. It's alive; but deceitful. It's a trap into which Kerguelen himself fell on his second voyage.

Each time he thinks he has reached land, it disappears from view. He thinks he is the victim of a hoax. In a letter to his patron the duc de Croÿ, he complains of the bad weather he has had since he reached the fortieth parallel. "One can truthfully say that it was by dint of gales combined with cold, snow, mists, and ice that I finally sighted my lands on 14 December 1773." His lands! He speaks of them as a Breton squire would, referring to his farms and his fields of rye. Actually, this possessive should be regarded as grimly ironical and even somewhat pathetic. The second voyage has been a disaster since the beginning. To add to his woes, Kerguelen is suffering from a bad case of erysipelas.

The archipelago is officially claimed for the second time on 6 January 1774. Kerguelen is evasive in the way he records the event in his *Account of Two Voyages in the Southern Seas and India*. He doesn't even mention the name of the officer who went ashore. The operation was led by Monsieur de Rochegude, an officer of the *Oiseau*, under the command of Monsieur de Rosnevet. Kerguelen simply notes that the said Rosnevet's men "had killed several penguins and sea lions on the sand: and that the captain 'had taken possession of this bay and all the land in the name of the King of France with all due formality.'"

Does it hurt him not to have carried out the act himself? Nothing seems to interest him. He doesn't bother to find out if these lands are islands or a continent. He didn't even see the Arched Rock of Kerguelen. A sailor on board the *Roland*, Ensign Pagès, caught sight of it. This man is his worst enemy, who will testify against him at the trial. He is the first person to mention "a carriage entrance through which one can see daylight" and christens it "the Portal." Its name will be given to a cape (*pointe du Portail*), but only for a short time.[3] Calling an arch over 330 feet high "a carriage entrance" is evidence of a small mind. Moreover those who knew him said that Pagès was a fool.

At the end of his letter to the duc de Croÿ, Kerguelen finally decides to tell the truth. "The southern lands we have sailed around do not appear to have any resources. They are nearly all covered in snow. All we have seen on land are sea wolves,[4] penguins, and other sea birds. There is no indication that the country is inhabited." One can imagine that this admission must have been painful, but also something of a relief. Once there is an admission, there is a misdeed. Does Kerguelen already sense the disgrace and humiliation he will have to endure in Brest?

Cook will have better luck. The two ships in his third voyage around the world, the *Resolution* and the *Discovery*, left Plymouth on 12 July 1776, reaching the Desolation Islands on 24 December 1776. Cook is on his last voyage—he will be killed in Hawaii—and does not come across these islands by chance. He knows that they were discovered by a Breton gentleman, Kerguelen. This land intrigues him. He knows nothing about the second voyage the Frenchman made three years previously. Kerguelen will later lay great stress on the bad weather to exonerate himself, but Cook must have had to contend with it too. But it's an established fact that when the English navigator reached the coast of Kerguelen, the wind dropped. For the whole week of his stay there, the archipelago had really balmy weather.

Cook's ship, the *Resolution*, lands in the northwest of the archipelago, entering the same Oiseau Bay as Kerguelen. Whereas Rochegude's small open boat had faced all sorts of danger trying to land, the Englishmen's boat glides over still water and has no trouble at all pulling into shore. It's the twenty-fifth of December 1776. Cook decides to call this grey beach with a few penguins trotting about on it Christmas Harbor (*Port-Christmas*). The name has remained.

He then discovers the basalt arch. "A high rock which is perforated quite through so as to appear like the arch of a bridge. We did not see such another on the whole coast."[5] He christens the point Arched Rock. That name has also been kept.

Cook is the first man to officially give a name to the towering black arch. It's significant that he should have immediately thought of the arch of a bridge. Yet this bridge doesn't link anything; it's built against thin air. Cook sensed the enigma of this structure standing alone, spanning nothing but empty space.

In the evening of 27 December, one of the men on the expedition rushed up waving a bottle he found wedged in a rock on the northern shore of the bay. Cook uncorks it and smoothes out the document inside. The message is in Latin:

Lucovico XV Galliarum
Rege et d. de Boynes
Regis a Secretis ad res
Maritimas annis 1772 et 1773.

Cook had only known about Kerguelen's first voyage. He thinks he is at the spot where Boisguehenneuc had landed. Now the bottle had obviously been left by Rochegude. Cook puts the parchment back in the bottle, drops in a two-penny piece dated 1772, seals the lead cap on the neck and insists on going himself the following day to lay the flask on a cairn, close to where it had been found.[6] He then goes up to the top of French Cape and retains an impression of "sterility in the highest degree."

During the days that follow, Cook recognizes some headlands on the north coast and proceeds up to the entrance of Royal Pass. With his infallible flair, he concludes that the Kerguelens are not one continent, as their discoverer had thought, but an island of no great size: "which from its sterility I shall call the Island Desolation."

The account of his third voyage was published after his death and is not entirely authentic. It contains additions made by its editor, Canon Douglas. This dignitary of St Paul's Cathedral inserts some of his own thoughts in the text. He ventures to add the following detail: "which from its sterility, I should, with great propriety, call the Island of Desolation, but that I would not rob Monsieur de Kerguelen of the honor of its bearing his name."

So, if the islands bear Kerguelen's name, it's really due to a none too scrupulous prelate. Like America, Kerguelen was not named by a navigator but by a scholar. At least this manipulative canon was fair-minded. Added to that, it was more through laziness and above all indifference that the name of Kerguelen was finally adopted at the end of the nineteenth century. For a long time English and American whalers still continued calling them the Desolation Islands.

A wash drawing by Weber, a companion of Cook and an illustrator of some repute, shows the two ships at anchor on the waters of a lagoon. This is Christmas Harbor with the Arch in the background. Its black Cyclops eye seems to have calmed the waters. There is a kind of grace in Cook's brief visit to the Desolation Islands in such incredibly good weather that highlights Kerguelen's bad luck and failure. While the Frenchman tacks laboriously around the archipelago with his two heavy ships, the Englishman skims around the coast making one or two casual sorties on land. He takes it all in and understands it at first glance, but he is already beginning to think ahead, forgetting the islands and heading straight for New Zealand. His daring and determination are already there in the names of his two ships: the *Discovery* and the *Resolution*, originally built as coal ships. The master of the *Resolution* was none other than William Bligh, the future captain of the *Bounty*. Cook quite liked a joke and gave the name Bligh's Cap to what is now known as Rendez-vous Islet to the north of the island because it looked like his second-in-command's hat.

The name chosen for a ship is never free of connotation. The *Gros-Ventre*, which takes possession of the land for the first time in 1772, may well bear the name of a bird, but all one remembers is its lumpish, plump but also expansive side. It will have less bad luck than the other vessel, a store ship. It is well named: the *Fortune*. The French word means luck, either good or bad. As it happened, Kerguelen's luck was bad. The crew won't see a thing of Desolation Island, just like the captain who seems to have approached "his lands" blindfolded.

The *Gros-Ventre* continues on its way east looking for the mysterious Gonneville Land. A month later, it sights land covered with sand dunes: it's the west coast of Australia. France arrives there before the English and will continue to claim it for part of the nineteenth century.

3

The days go by in Travers Valley, but it's hard to keep track of them. The present usually maintains the symmetry between past and future; here it wavers like a balance beam on a weighing machine. My friends have talked me out of leaving on my own. I should wait until they have taken all their samples. I've imagined the Arch so much that I fear the huge pierced rock of my dreams might one day collapse.

In the late afternoon I usually take a bath in the thermal pool. The skua regularly keeps me company a few yards from my bathtub. He stays watching me for hours, unconcerned by the sudden gestures I make to chase him away. When I get up to go back to the cabin, he trots behind me as though he were afraid of losing me.

He hasn't come today. Getting out of the bath, I try to guess where he might be and wander about without paying much attention to the fading light. I come across a stream I haven't seen before behind some fallen rock: I'm lost. I have to come back towards the thermal springs where I can easily get my bearing to return to the cabin. But the hot springs have disappeared too. The swirls of steam, which can usually be seen from a long way off, seem to have evaporated.

I think I recognize a rock that looks like the pointed helmet of a Scythian warrior; in fact there seems to be an army of rocks facing me in the shadows, ready to attack. Their helmets have gleaming spots of mica or smudges of rust.

Twilight crashes down on the day rather than falls, and the stunning effect is like a building being demolished by implosion. The growing darkness now brings out whitish spots on the mottled stone warriors.

All the shapes come to life. The basalt seems to regain the volcanic violence of its origins and begin moving. Its sooty color should blend in with the darkness, but the rock shakes and rises up, gleaming in the night like glassy, glistening fissures in coal.

I try to find my way among the statues. They move forward the moment I turn my back.

I soon come out in the bottom of ravine surrounded by an almost vertical wall. The darkness is slowly, rather hesitantly coming towards me.

The wall is riddled with cavities and the evening wind wails a lament as it blows into them. I seem to detect a note of mocking, even hatred in these moaning voices. I try to get out of the ravine. I know now that I won't find the cabin.

The landscape around me doesn't look like anything now: just shattered stone slabs, fallen rock, holes. The black water shines like Indian ink.

My friends back in the cabin have no doubt gone out to look for me. Calling out is no help: the swirling wind would stifle the sound of my voice.

Feeling my way around the wall, I find a break in the side of the cliff. The night wraps around me like black velvet, but not to keep me warm. The temperature has fallen.

It's as cold as the tomb in my cave. The wind can sing away in my ears as much as it likes, I'm still shivering and feeling very much alone.

I have to go outside. My eyes are now used to the dark and I can make out shadows.

In the distance I can hear a waterfall, like the rumbling of a train doing a fast switch. It's a long, continuous sound.

Then I catch sight of a tiny glimmer down below far away

in the dark. It moves, disappears then comes up again brighter than before.

The sky, which had grown overcast at sunset, clears in places, revealing a constellation of stars. Their reflection shimmers on the water of some river or on the surface of a mud pool.

That dying light intrigues me. Why is there only one twinkling light while there are numerous stars visible in the sky? The gleam wavers between blue and red. As I walk farther down, it becomes a purple color. I think I must be one or two miles from the light. It's impossible to walk straight towards it because of the very uneven terrain.

I fall over several times, causing a fall of stones that bounce off into the night. Having gone around an outcrop taking me away from my path, I can't see the will-o-the-wisp any more. I retrace my steps, but the escarpment that prevented me from passing a moment ago has also disappeared.

Solitude has crept up on me in the dark. I can touch it, it hits me like the stones I keep tripping over. It's so palpable that it suddenly stops frightening me. Since I decided not to give way to the illusions of the dark, I feel calm, almost happy.

To keep my spirits up, I think of John Nunn, the Robinson Crusoe of Kerguelen. During a whaling expedition, this English sailor was shipwrecked and abandoned on Kerguelen with three companions. They survived by wearing sealskin and eating sea elephants and penguin eggs. Like prehistoric men, they jealously kept their fire burning in seal oil. They threw messages into the sea using albatross gall. They captured birds and attached a notice to their backs. It became quite a game. There are some pastimes that can save a man.

The four Robinson Crusoes had to wait for two years before being picked up by a whaler that had just begun its tour, which meant that they had to live another two years on these islands. Unlike the original Robinson, who had tools and provisions, John Nunn had only a musket and a copy of *Young's Night Thoughts*. I try to imagine myself declaiming Pope's verses for two years. In a situation like that, one must become attached to any kind of book.

When every protection has failed, when one can only rely on what there is inside oneself, could the book one hasn't chosen be the book that will save? Robinson Crusoe had a Bible, which was more precious to him than his tools and his musket. He liked to open it at random, lucidly interpreting the most insignificant verse like a message sent from heaven.

Any book has meaning for a survivor. Its contents are not of great importance. The slightest story is stimulating because it creates the illusion of being free. We are no longer alone. Something that under ordinary circumstances might seem obscure or insignificant takes on new meaning. The mind brought down to essentials can immediately extract the essence of things, elucidate what is impenetrable, provide what is lacking. With almost nothing one can invent almost everything.

Suddenly the light bursts out in front of me, much brighter. It flickers like embers being set alight by the wind. I feel as though I'm leaving the gates of Hell behind me. I mustn't look back.

The light draws closer, bursting through the clouds in a suddenly bright sky. The white moon now lights up the stream, the dale, and the cabin. The sometimes violet light comes from a butane lamp.

The imagination will always be quelled by butane gas.

My sudden appearance scarcely disturbs my friends' comfortable silence. Georges is preparing the meal. The soup is bubbling on the little stove, giving off a lovely smell of bacon and vegetables. The lamp hisses quietly. The man in the parka is lying on his mattress reading *The Sheet Anchor*. The third is fiddling with his camera.

Was I really lost? It's eight o'clock.... Only three hours since I left for the hot springs. I was sure I'd lived through twice that. One of them asks me if I've had a good walk: "We were almost beginning to get worried...."

4

We leave Travers Valley a little before dawn under a pale yellow sky streaked with trails of filmy black floating above the valley. The wind pounds them against the hillsides. It tries to imitate the noise of the thunder with its dull booms rolling on into distant gorges, which turns them into a kind of harsh but indistinct growl as they echo round and round their walls.

The glow of sulfur and black ash in the sky deepens as the day breaks. I don't want to look at the cabin behinds me. "But Lot's wife looked back behind him, and she became a pillar of salt." (Genesis)

We want to reach Armor, where there is an experimental

salmon farm. Armor is situated at the end of the very deep lake we went past at the beginning of our trip. The lighter, the *Aventure*, brings supplies from Port aux Français twice a week. This time we have decided to take the shortest route. After walking for half an hour, we are stopped by a strongly flowing river, but we are determined to cross it, less to gain time than as a sort of challenge.

On contact with the icy water my feet feel as though they are burning, then it's my thighs. The burning acts like a cautery. The nerves are deadened and the flesh becomes numb. It's not unpleasant. The lack of feeling is actually rather sensual; a part of the body has become separate from the rest, giving a sensation of lightness. I push hard against the water in front of me. It's only on climbing out of the river that the shooting pain hits me.

There is flowing water everywhere in Kerguelen, forming an intricate network of little streams, rivers, and lakes that blend and intermingle. As the ground is impermeable, the water can't readily sink into it. These countless filaments often have their source in the peat bogs, which are a gigantic reservoir. Nonetheless, the dominion of water is challenged by air. A shower or a downpour can be immediately wiped out by the wind. A few blasts will soak up and absorb everything. After very heavy rain, the chaotic energy of creation shows its strength in Kerguelen to measure its strength against that seismic force; you have to hurry when it seems to be peaceful.

Once we have crossed the river, we start on the mountain, tackling its steepest side. The wind furiously batters the heights stretched tight like an ox hide. It's always the same sound: a low subterranean salvo as though the top of the mountain had been undermined and was about to explode. The waterfalls hurtling down its side suddenly dry up with the brutal force of the wind. Reduced to nothing by the squall, the flow of water is dispersed into particles that fly off like thousands of fireflies.

Light suddenly streams out between the clouds, and through the fine droplets of water, throwing a huge rainbow from the mountain to the valley. "It shall be, when I bring a cloud over the earth, that the rainbow shall be seen in the cloud; And I will remember My covenant which is between Me and you and every living creature of all flesh." (Genesis) The colors of the celestial arch are so clear that, when I hold out my hand towards the rainbow, a shower of gold and turquoise falls into my palm. The drops are pointed like diamonds and so cold that they scratch my skin and prick my hot face.

The wind is so icy that once I get to the top, I can't allow myself time to rest. It has chilled my sweating body in an instant. A dreary plateau stretches out in front of us. Mount Isolation (*le mont de la Solitude*) rises up out of it under a livid sky. Here, the place names and the landscape are definite and explicit. There are no gradations. Only a scientist would have the idea of calling this mountain *Isolation*.

How can you measure isolation or loneliness? By the friction that the slightest sound produces in the air: it vibrates wildly and repeatedly but doesn't communicate anything, then it dies. Isolation is a kind of thickness that pads and stifles sounds so that the only ones left are the sound of footsteps and one's own blood pulsing in the temples. I can hear it; it's a kind of acoustic darkness that falls on the landscape and reduces it to nothing. But this imprisonment of the sound wave has nothing to do with silence. Isolation has its own particular resonance. It's a slow slide into absence, an empty shuddering brought on by an unknown force. "Be silent, all flesh, before the Lord." (Zechariah)

The geologist Edgar Aubert de la Rüe gave that name to the mountain in 1928. He gave no explanation for his choice. "But," Delépine points out, "the name has the approval of the topographers, who thought one evening that the helicopter wouldn't be coming back to pick them up."

Aubert de la Rüe, who was born in 1901, was the great explorer of the Kerguelens between the First and Second World Wars. He was a precursor in the tradition of Bossières and Rallier du Baty, staying there several times between 1928 and 1953.

His wife accompanied him on all his voyages. They slept in a tent in the foulest weather. This native of Geneva, descended from a French family, was a strict, religious man who has been forgotten for the very reason of his moral rectitude.

You can't fault him in his book *Two years in the Desolation Islands*. He believed in nothing but facts. He had no time for the ignorant people who got off at Port aux Français and thought they had come to a virgin land. Yet the strangeness of Kerguelen disconcerted him.

This austere man loved the almost abstract severity of the Desolation Islands and their "infinite sadness." I wanted to look up Aubert de la Rüe, but could not find out whether he was still alive. I was told that he was living in seclusion in Lausanne and that he had lost his memory. However, during the service at Touffreville in honor of the Bossière brothers, the priest mentioned Aubert de la Rüe in his prayer for the dead. After that, I gave up my search.

The mud wallow sucks hard at our boots. It oozes from the ground like slime. Organic deposits form rust-colored strips that become a pale iridescent green. We can smell the stagnant water. It's like lactic acid, slightly sour, vaguely like beer, but so extraordinary that I imagine I'm smelling the primeval soup before it swelled and became more solid.

Kerguelen came from a volcano, yet the original explosion was not really so long ago. The world was never restored to what it was before that devastation. A scar has formed over the wound, but underneath it is still raw. I'm walking over bleeding, exhausted earth.

The wind howling in our ears is as unbearable as hearing the sobs of someone in pain. We have to make a stop halfway up a mountain, hardly able to stand because the squalls are so violent and we are being sucked into their vortex. The wind sets my face on fire, makes my clothes flap like bunting and pushes me downhill towards the twin lakes where the still waters are such a contrast to the wind's violent attack on us.

One is called Lake Tristan and the other, Lake Isolde. Down in the valley, the roar has given way to a deep voice that sounds like the bombardon organ stop. When the voice rises an octave, it imitates a trumpet. The wind has slowed down and become an organist practicing its scales on the basalt pipes, rippling up and down with supreme skill.

All the way down this gravel-covered valley, we are puzzled by a white shape in the distance. For a long time it hardly seems to move, but then gives a sudden leap. Is it a man or an animal? The white shape gives a jerk. It seems to be brandishing a stick above its head, unless it's a radio antenna. We can't explain its regular pattern of movements. As we draw closer, the jerking becomes more of a rise and fall. We walk faster, more and more intrigued.

Then we finally identify the shape: it's a solitary reindeer. Our presence doesn't frighten it. It's nevertheless a bit surprised and, above all, curious. It stands there at a safe distance, but instead of moving away, it sometimes ventures coming closer to inspect us.

Reindeer were introduced on two islands of the archipelago in 1955 and 1956: High Island and Main Island (*la Grande Terre*). As there was not enough room left on High Island and they had eaten the few lichens and the azorella (an umbelliferous plant that forms thick green or brown clumps in rock hollows), the reindeer swam across in 1975. They managed to cross the isthmus, which was about a mile wide, to rejoin the Main Island herd. It's thought they number about 3,000 today. Many of them die. The males are so taken up with rutting that they don't store the fat they need to survive the winter.

What is this reindeer doing so far from its herd? It looks us up and down, hesitates, then plunges into the water. It doesn't even bother to turn around to see if we are following and takes his time reaching the other side.

A river links Lake Tristan to Lake Isolde. The reindeer is now standing on the opposite bank. He's not entirely sure of us, preferring to put a little stream between us, which allows us to come closer. The reindeer follows us like that quite happily for two hours. We can see his beautiful, gentle, sad eyes. He has attached himself to us, and as we stand there admiring the size of his antlers, he slowly turns his head so that we can take our time admiring him.

Suddenly he's not there. We look all around for him. He reappears on top of a hill, standing there in the sunset looking huge and almost frightening. He's not the familiar animal he was before, but an unknown, mythical beast, a sort of austral unicorn, a motionless, threatening god barring our way. The fork of his enormous antlers in the glow of the evening light seems to be on fire. The moist slit below its eyes seems huge. This tear gland sparkles, sending out disturbingly steady flashes of light. The rays of the sun concentrated on the apparition, like the mysterious stag always hunted but untouchable, are the only source of light at that moment. It's as though the monstrous animal had deliberately placed himself at the top of the hill to inspire fear. I quicken my pace, not daring to turn my head, feeling those black eyes watching my back.

Night has fallen and I feel reassured. We pitch our tent against a low bank protected from the wind by clumps of acaena. As I lie there half awake and half asleep, the regular ebb and flow of the sea seems to imitate the sound of the rising wind. At daybreak I go out and spread my sleeping bag on the sand now damp from the night air. When I'm finally falling asleep gazing at the sea, the surface of the water suddenly rises and churns. Two dark shapes leap out, so powerful and unexpected that for a moment I think my drowsy mind must have imagined them. They are Commerson dolphins, recognizable by their very large black heads and their rounded pectoral fins. They dive straight down and come up again whistling as they leap. Their pearly bodies swirling with fine drops of water quiver in the morning air. The patterns of their dance draw perfectly regular lines of foam on the surface of the water, which disappear very, very slowly. There is something childlike in the way they keep composing a message so gracefully in an unknown alphabet.

5

Armor in the distance. The power plant, the circular fish-breeding ponds, the sheds, the workshops hidden between the lake and the sea have the look of some secret base set up in the middle of a stony desert by a mad scientist. Strangely enough, these modern constructions blend into the landscape fairly well. The site seems to have been half demolished at some stage, taken apart then suddenly left as it was before the destruction was complete. Smashed rock and blocks of stone with rounded edges pave the ground, full of irregular shaped bumps. What creates this hidden harmony between a haphazard heap of megaliths and these new constructions? Water. It gives a sense of calm and order to the landscape, which looks like a corner of Brittany. The marine farm is in a valley filled by a lake. It flows out into a fjord and would remind one of some quiet canning factory if it weren't for the unusually still waters of the lake. A floating raft looks like the box of a camera obscura as the water captures the landscape without the slightest ripple disturbing the picture.

The green of the acaena growing on the slopes, the slate blue of the Devil's Volcano, the red basalt layers of rock are reflected on the black water in soft watercolor tones. There is something cheerful about this muted glow. The Breton word *armor* means *sea country*, and this armor breaks the endless and incurable melancholy that hangs over so much of the Kerguelen landscape.

An ocean farm: here at last is a southland dream come to fruition! Chickens scratch about for food in the yard in company with the skuas. These carrion birds generally keep their distance and a beating of wings will chase them away when they try to take the food meant for the poultry yard. Water is flowing in the ponds with a quiet whisper I'd forgotten about. This water is *civilized*, controlled by man, as opposed to the ungovernable streams of water that pour over the ground in Kerguelen. The slippery bodies of the young fish quiver in the tanks.

It's late. I see someone at the entrance to the living quarters. He's leaning over to pull off his boots and put on his slippers. I find this homely gesture quite touching.

"I told you we'd meet again," the man says, putting his index finger inside the back of the slipper to pull up the heel. I don't recognize him straight away. He's not wearing his Basque beret. He's the one who welcomed me when I landed at Port aux Français. My companions greet him enthusiastically.

The interior is furnished with two armchairs covered in leatherette, a couch and an amazing Normandy-style sideboard. Heavy chairs in the pseudo-German medieval style dear to those who live in the faubourg Saint-Antoine in Paris take up most of the room. This petty bourgeois salon seems the height of refinement and comfort.

The Armor base, situated twenty-five miles west of Port aux Français at the end of the Morbihan Gulf, was set up in 1983 to acclimatize salmon to Kerguelen. Four VATs (volunteer technicians) live there the whole year, looking after the fish farming installations, the power plant, and the pumping station. The site was chosen because of the short outfall between Lake Armor and the sea, which permits a regulated flow and good guidance for the returning salmon.

We have a river char with pale pink, full-flavored flesh for dinner. "A Kerguelen char," the man with the Basque beret announces with pride. He tells the story of this fish introduced into the archipelago with the trout in 1955. The fresh waters of the Kerguelens have a low level of mineralization, are poor in food salts, and have only a few small crustaceans living in them. The absence of predators favored the reproduction of the newly introduced species. The char, which likes deep, pure water, is slowly disappearing from the lakes in Savoie and Switzerland; on the other hand, they thrive in Kerguelen. Before living species disappear one after the other from the face of our planet, perhaps they will find refuge in this Noah's ark floating in the middle of the vast southern ocean. Its oblivion will ensure the continuity of life on earth.

If a nuclear war destroyed the whole of Europe and America, Desolation Island would be one of places in the world best protected from radioactive fallout. I've often heard the men of winter mission say, "Kerguelen is the best atomic shelter," as if to convince themselves that absolute isolation is a privilege. A young geophysicist taking samples of CO_2 in the atmosphere, who is visiting Armor, explains that the pattern of air circulation makes the atmospheric microparticles avoid Kerguelen and tend to fall in the tropical latitudes or on the Antarctic coast.

We try to imagine the human race wiped out all over the earth apart from the archipelago, which has been safe from nuclear fire.

"Let's throw in a few conjectures. What would happen?" Georges asks.

"The survivors would have an extension of time," I suggest, "but man would disappear because there are no women."

The discussion becomes much more lively at this point. Someone points out that two or three women scientists stay here for several months during the summer mission.

"If the cataclysm happened during that time, what would happen then?" Georges says, wanting an answer to his question.

One of us thinks that once the shock of the nuclear holocaust had passed, the mission would close ranks. But who would get the women? The VAT in the parka is sure they would choose their men just as they had always done since Eve. It would be a fierce contest. The return of the horde. It's likely that the chief would take the three women for himself. But would the sixty other survivors accept that?

Who would be the chief of the survivors?

"In the beginning, I think it would be the *disker*," Georges says.

"The *disker!*" I'm really surprised, wondering why it would be the disc jockey.

"Yes, the *disker!* That's what we call him here. It's short for head of the Kerguelen district (*dis-ker*).

Now I realize my mistake. The confident man with the walkie-talkie I saw when I arrived is the official representing the administration.

"After a while," says Georges, "we would probably have to kill the *disker*."

We don't agree, and I ask him why.

"Because he represents the old order, the father figure," Georges replies. "You know that any group has to commit a common crime to survive."

It sounds as though Georges has read Freud. It's strange, this Kerguelen tendency to invent a beginning, perhaps because the real beginnings have always failed. The volume rises. We now consider the possibility of dividing the archipelago into rival principalities: one with Port aux Français as the capital, and Armor the other. Someone cites the example of John Nunn, the man who was shipwrecked on Kerguelen. Like Robinson Crusoe, he had set up several "homes" on the island. With his three companions, he built Hope Cottage, to the east of here in what is now the Courbet Peninsula. The house was built with blocks of peat. The four men had put up lots of signs and symbols, to maintain the illusion that they hadn't lost contact with the other world. Not only had they built a little windmill, but it also served as a weathercock.

When you have lost everything, you can create abundance in your mind; possession has only ever been a matter of the imagination. In point of fact, a free man doesn't possess anything. This endless frustration is the price of freedom. A person who is shipwrecked—or a prisoner—has a rarer privilege: he has a higher mastery and enjoyment of the most trifling things. He can create a whole world from a book, a piece of metal, a landscape, from himself. In the history of Desolation Island, only Nunn and his companions succeeded in *possessing* it. They opened it out, like unrolling a map, always being so careful to make the most of everything possible that, one day, they managed to make use of something unlikely.

This something unlikely turns up in the shape of a young sea elephant that had been wounded by a spear. Who threw it? There's someone on the island. This spear wound is the sign of human life Robinson discovers by chance on the beach. The crew of a whaler is hunting on the coast. The shipwrecked men eventually join up with it.

The man with the Basque beret belongs to a strange species. He is a voluntary castaway on Kerguelen. He is a representative of a tribe that has only a few members: The Kerguelians, a hybrid race, a crossbreed from the scientific species, resulting in a kind of southern-ocean bushman. The Kerguelian is passionately attached, not to the land, but to something new and mysterious. Some strange call urges him to keep coming back. He's an active contemplative. He will often give up an excellent scientific career in his home country to devote himself entirely to observing and understanding the Desolation Islands. The man in the beret is a hydrobiologist. He came to the archipelago for the first time in 1969. It was his idea to introduce salmon to Kerguelen and set up a marine farm.

"For a long time, Armor was like a ball-and-chain," he confesses.

His calmness and his energy make me think of Captain Nemo. He may not be as stern as Jules Verne's hero, but he is driven by the obsession: conquer the sea and make it bring back his salmon. His *Nautilus* is Armor.

The Kerguelen Islands haunt the works of Jules Verne. The author of *Twenty Thousand Leagues under the Sea*, who was obsessed by confinement (ships, caves, islands), knew the archipelago well. He writes about it at length in his book *The Great Navigators of the Eighteenth Century*, and defends the Chevalier de Kergeulen.

In *The Mysterious Island*, six people are stranded on an unknown island not unlike Kerguelen. It's very jagged, isolated, and empty. This last point is important, as the native issue is nonexistent. In the beginning, the survivors are afraid of this chaos, but their lives are transformed when they decide to give names to headlands, promontories, rivers, and mountains.

"They set up a village that is something like Armor," the man in the Basque beret says, rather ironically.

"Yes, and near the outlet, like Armor. They dry out the lake and build *Granite House*. You see... You haven't been the first to do it."

"But real life is less romantic than the novels of Jules Verne. Armor is part of a research project set up at the request of the TAAF department (French Southern and Antarctic Territories). It's not a pipe dream, even though salmon is fairly cheap everywhere these days. Given Kerguelen's remoteness, raising it here is not a profitable operation. But when water pollution in Europe or the Pacific reaches a critical level and the survival of the salmon there is threatened, Armor will perhaps come into its own."

Some VATs have joined us. They came to Armor four months ago. Their winter duty will be finished in eight months' time. Apart from his work in the marine farm, each "Armorigine," as they are called, has taken on a household chore. You would think it was a workers' commune. Everyone realizes his own dream. In a way, Armor does away with the division between work and play. One of them admits that a year ago he didn't know that Kerguelen existed.

"I feel like a survivor. I'm already thinking about going home. I'll never be the same after this year at Armor."

"Is it so hard here?"

"Oh no. It's going back to France that will be hard."

6

The supply boat *Aventure*, which was to take me back to Port aux Français, hasn't been able to get under way because of bad weather. Desolation Island, a land of waiting. Waiting for the supply boat, waiting for a better weather report, waiting for the *Marion*, waiting for the Arch that I couldn't reach from Travers Valley. It's hope without the impatience. Each day is so much like the last that you become confused and time means nothing. How many days have I been at Armor? Three, four? Events don't follow each other chronologically; they drift unchecked, depending on the weather forecast.

Time is a space that the sky and the wind leave open. There

is no need to fill this gap. Waiting doesn't exhaust itself in useless exertion or in pathetic signs we are usually so anxious to
interpret. There is an indolence in Kerguelian idleness that is
the opposite of apathy: it's a kind of fervently happy-go-
lucky attitude, without an object. The mind is not dependent
on either facts or moments; it is not a prisoner of the past or
the future. There is no order of days. Kerguelians never say,
"Today is Monday (or Tuesday)." The present means nothing: the days of the week are all the same.

You don't "kill" time in Kerguelen and you don't "fool" it.
It's not a tyrant, but a nice companion, discrete and obliging,
who doesn't like people paying attention to it.

As I don't have to wait for anything, I set out this morning
for the Devil's Volcano. I've been dying to explore this mountain that has blasted open, leaving a yawning crater spilling out
thousands of black stones. The climb is easy on the huge slag
heap. As I go farther, the pumicite gives out a hollow metallic
ring when I step on it. From time to time, large pieces of the
slag heap give way. I don't seem to be making any progress.

The summit is a promontory that dominates the whole
southern part of the central plateau and reveals unknown
horizons as far as the eye can see. Gulfs, islets, rivers, and
lakes sparkle beneath the most extraordinary light effects.
Every shade of blue, grey, and gold is spread out before you.
It's all haloes, glories, nimbuses, streams of light that look as
though they could have come from a book of holy pictures
illustrating some epiphany or assumption into heaven.

I'm at the center of a painted fan. A delicate mist wafts back
and forth, opening and shutting the ends as if it were playing

games with me. Real cliffs, false headlands, imaginary peaks—where is reality? The misty sea winding its way between the archipelagos creates domes and cupolas over the islands. All strength and power is in the wind. The strength of the wind that crinkles the sea into row upon row of white crests all along the coast; the liveliness of the light that changes completely from one moment to the next, revealing unknown bays with a complicated series of inlets reaching out into the sea like fingers.

The regular flow of air from the bellows of the universe cleanses the air so vigorously that the bluish stones shine as though they were as transparent as a sapphire.

A mound of stones has been hastily put together on the slate gray plateau. It's certainly the work of human hands. I even know how many stones there are: about fifty. There is a custom handed on by the Armor people to those who reach the top of the Devil's Volcano: they should add their stone to the pyramid. It brings you back to reality and calls for humility. This pile of pebbles puts any traveler who might claim to be the first one there back in his proper place.

Between the blank page and the finished book, Kerguelen creates the illusion of being close to its origins or its end. Travelers have been disappointed to discover they were neither the first nor the only ones to come here. For example, many ships came to Kerguelen for the Transit of Venus in 1874. The captain of the American ship, the *Charles Coldgate*, was quite put out when he realized that Kerguelen was "so well-known."

As I go down again towards Armor, there is a damp, mineral smell in the wind coming from pebbles that have been wet by a passing squall. It's not like the sea; it's more the rarefied air of the mountain tops mixed with humus and flint—lively and slightly sour. Desolation's stones give off an unusual, strong odor, a very definite smell of ore and gunflint: the smell of a living, brooding land. No other smell has any effect on it.

PART THREE

Port Jeanne d'Arc

"Deliver me out of the mire, and let me not sink."

Psalm 69, v. 14.

I

In spite of a heavy swell, the *Aventure* left Port Aux Français for Armor this morning. It was able to pull alongside the quay near the dam. The supply lighter, which plies up and down the Morbihan Gulf, took just enough time to throw some provisions on the landing stage then left straight away for Port Jeanne d'Arc. After that it will deliver some scientific equipment to several islands. This holdup might mean that I can't go to Christmas Harbor.

This is the first time I realize that the present is not going to last forever and the end of my stay is approaching.

I barely have time to throw my bag on deck and grab the ship's rail. The boat pulls out from the quay at full speed with the propeller violently churning the sea, raising billows of foam full of seaweed.

I find Captain Couesnon on board plus the group of seven parachutists who boarded the *Marion* with me at Réunion. They are going to set up a backup camp in the ruins of Port Jeanne d'Arc. They will use it as a base for a long-distance reconnaissance towards the south of the island.

The boat goes by Guillou Island, which bears the name of a sailor who died on Kerguelen in 1966. Through the fine rain, the bronze basalt rocks gleam with light, just like the interwoven iron links in a coat of mail. The parachutists are standing silently and still on deck, braving the wind and the rain. I can see their hooded heads from the bridge where I've taken shelter. Standing there close together at the prow of the boat, gazing gloomily at the horizon, they look like medieval warriors.

A hand suddenly emerges from a raincoat, pointing to a distant heap of metal and wooden planks and a dotted line of huts.They are the ruins of the Port Jeanne d'Arc whaling station. "Péjida!" exclaims the *Aventure*'s quartermaster. For the moment, I don't understand what he means. It's actually the abbreviation of Port Jeanne d'Arc (PJDA). The Kerguelians love various types of abbreviation, such as *manip*, *disker,* and *appro.*

The boat moves as close to the island as it can, but we have to wade ashore. The soldiers get the trunks, packs, and bags on to the beach in a few minutes. The *Aventure* is already underway again. Heaven knows when it will return to take me back to the Port aux Français base. The helicopter is my last chance to get to Christmas Harbor.

Two buildings are still standing. One is in good condition; the other is held up only by part of the collapsed roof that supports the walls. The rest of the framework has been pushed over by the wind, flattening everything as it fell. The parachutists have decided to stay at Port Jeanne d'Arc for several days and invite me to take advantage of the shelter they are going to build. Chief Warrant Officer Le Lay is squat and not given to unnecessary movement. He is also an experienced cook. He made sure to pack ingredients that are impossible to find on Kerguelen: garlic, onions, and curry.

The wooden hut has been built in Scandinavian style, which is not surprising as Port Jeanne d'Arc was set up in 1908–1909 by a company made up mainly of Norwegians. The firm Storm Bull, established in the Cape, had acquired the right to hunt whales in Kerguelen from the Bossière brothers.

The Norwegians called the factory station Port Jeanne d'Arc to honor France. Protected by Long Island and sheltered from the west wind by high hills, the settlement was established to receive whales that had been caught and to render down their fat in autoclaves. Today it is a huge heap of wooden slats and rusty vats. All that is left of the wooden wharf connected to the buildings by Decauville tracks are two sections that are about to collapse into the sea. Although their roofing has been torn off, a few constructions still resist the devastation the wind wreaks on the ruins. The wind purrs like a big cat, but starts growling when anyone decides to fill in a hole or rearrange the iron sheets hanging down from the windows like dead birds.

At one stage, the whaling station housed up to 140 people. Our hut was meant for staff: the next house was for the manager, who came from Christiania (Oslo).

The base of a settee or a sofa has shrunk almost as much as it can, dried out by the strong wind. It's all shriveled up canvas and cut edges. The Aeolian fire has withered everything. All that remains of a dismembered stove is the cast-iron soleplate.

Yet there is nothing depressing about these ruins. The shaking boards and the iron sheets hang like garlands moving this way and that in the wind. They quiver like leaves on a tree. This debris is alive. The wind that dries and destroys can also preserve and renew. The rain that stains, pits, and rusts has made wonderful blends of red-brown and orange on the metal. Corrosion has pierced the whale oil barrels with holes. They give the wind a voice. It booms like an organ and sounds a wild toccata with all stops out.

I spend the night in a bunk bed that has been there since the Norwegian days. It's a kind of wooden box as narrow as a coffin, which goes well with my sarcophagus sleeping bag. I can hear the night voices singing through the old door frames. Pebbles click-clack over wood. The woodwork groans and the floors creak with the force of the wind. *Péjida* seems about to burst apart.

I look around the ruins of the whaling station with Captain Couesnon. Port Jeanne d'Arc appears like the ghost towns you see in westerns. It's all rusty pipes, nails, iron stakes, hoops, and cables. Metal ingots are still tied in bundles as if a huge shipwreck had thrown everything up on the shore.

You can still see the slope where the whales were hauled up by steam winches. The posts, hardened and bleached by wind and rain, look like truncated marble columns. There is something about the way things are piled up here, as though men's efforts never managed to reach their full potential. Hence the lack of pathos.

In the midst of all this disorder stand the bulky cylinders of the autoclave vats.

"Everything will have collapsed in two years time," the captain predicts. "The only things intact are the tankers where the whale oil was stored." The captain is able to identify the workshop and the forge. Even though he is seeing Port Jeanne d'Arc for the first time as I am, he has an admirable knowledge of the way the whaling factory was set up. He digs about in the earth and finds joints and bolts.

"They made spare parts here. You can still find them. Not everything has been pilfered."

He points ruefully to the dismantled machines where everything has been taken including the copper plaques that showed the brand name and where it came from. Even the window frames have been taken down. Everything has been torn to pieces: a typically French practice of dismembering a place to get a souvenir. But pillage is not enough; you have to leave your signature. *Péjida*'s sheets of metal and planks of wood are covered with graffiti left by generations of people on winter duty. All these happy predators must look nostalgically at the paperweight or ashtray on their desk made out of bits pulled off a piece of equipment.

When he came back to Port Jeanne d'Arc in 1950 after an absence of twenty years, Aubert de la Rüe found to his surprise that there was German graffiti. They were names of sailors from the German raider *Komet*, which illicitly came to Kerguelen in 1941 to change camouflage. The Germans went ashore at Port Jeanne d'Arc and took away galvanized steel tubes, valves, cables, paint, rivets, bolts, etc., as well as petrol and 150 tons of anthracite.

The best remains of the whaling factory were fortunately too heavy or too cumbersome to be stolen. A millstone at least six feet in diameter lies near the autoclaves. It's so finely cut in four that you would think they were lines etched by the weather. The wind and rain have dented the polished surface, carving strange checkered patterns like an Aztec stone calendar.

A broken propeller lies on the ground a little farther on. The blades have been cut off in the middle. Why does Captain Couesnon talk of a "shattered dream"? The meteorite lying amid the ruins is like the dead soul of Port Jeanne d'Arc.

Yves de Kerguelen, the Bossière brothers, and Rallier du Baty were men who paid little attention to reality. They realized that Kerguelen could only exist through the power of illusion. Rallier du Baty alone succeeded in eluding that trap. He wisely devoted the rest of his life to research, "secretly living with his memories."[1] Dying at the age of ninety-seven, he is the only one for whom the adventure turned out well. What is more, he always found himself in Kerguelen at the right time. He was there, almost by chance, when Port Jeanne d'Arc was established, as he relates in his book.

Rallier tells how he and his five companions had been living alone on Kerguelen for ten months. One day when he is exploring a river with a member of the crew called Agnès, he notices smoke in the distance. It's a boat. As Agnès has been suffering for several days because the tobacco has run out, he rows towards it with an energy fuelled by despair, but the two men can't reach the unknown ship. They give up, feeling sick at heart. Imagine their surprise the next day when they get back to the *J.-B.-Charcot* and find the steamship moored beside it. It's the *Jeanne d'Arc* under the command of Captain Ring, who is looking for a site for his whaling factory. The Norwegian boat has a sack of mail on board. Rallier is delighted.

"We were like Rip van Winkles come back to life after a

long sleep, or prisoners who have spent a long time shut up in sepulchral silence being released and hearing everything that has happened in the world since they were taken from it."

In the days that follow, the Norwegians can't get over the tiny size of the *J.-B.-Charcot*. How could such a frail boat take the Frenchmen so far? They ask Rallier if he thinks the site for Port Jeanne d'Arc is a good choice.

"It's excellent. The beach is good and there is a freshwater stream but—and this 'but' seemed to worry them—I fear you won't find any whales in the Royal Channel (the entry to Morbihan Gulf).This news upset them and they later found it to be true."

The whales in the Kerguelens are found near Irish Bay, not far from Travers Valley. Rallier tells how one day he came upon such a big pod of whales that "the sea was black with their backs and fins." He goes on to say, "They were all blowing, and wherever we looked, we could see the sun reflected on their long, smooth bodies."

The whale boats can still be seen in the ruins of Port Jeanne d'Arc. These light, fast boats that were attached to the sides of the whaling ship now lie on their sides near the shore. By a strange mimesis, they have ended up resembling their victims. They look like a pod of sperm whales beached on the sand. The boats, which belly out in the middle and come to a point at each end so that they can maneuver from the front as well as from the back, have been wasting away here for eighty years. Just as the whales were sliced up on this very spot, the weather cuts the keel into pieces. The wind has carved them up, leaving most like skeletons. Many of the crosspieces of the hull are missing. The sides are milky white with more or less regular parasol-shaped flower clusters growing on them. When a whale dies and the water it blows is tinted with blood, it's customary for the sailors to say, "roses are red." The intertwining porcelain white roses on the boats in the Port Jeanne d'Arc cemetery lend a delicate touch to the rather ugly disorder.

The captain looks thoughtful as he says, "The whaling station was certainly the most modern of its day. Five years later, it was already out of date: the factory ships were becoming more profitable. Port Jeanne d'Arc's fate was meteoric. The firm Storm Bull went out of business in 1913. The only people left at the station were two caretakers, who were recalled in 1914."

Apart from rubbish left by successive visitors to Port Jeanne d'Arc, the whaling station isn't really dirty. The wind is a great cleaner. It scrapes, empties, rubs until it almost excises the substance out of the wood. The wooden boards are so light they seem to have been hollowed out. They disintegrate in sheets. The rain has polished any roughness but accentuated the veins, knots, and gnarls. All the lines washed by the rain form rosettes. Some knots have popped out leaving a perfectly rounded hole in the middle of the board.

Rubbish hidden amid the ruins has freeze-dried. When it rains, cardboard boxes and pieces of paper regain some of the shape they used to have. They have become rubbish artifacts, imitations of detritus free of its dirt. Port Jeanne d'Arc's refuse is the cleanest in the world.

Our hut has a few comforts: wooden tables, gas, provisions, and even running water that comes from the waterfall close by through pipes joined end to end. The water escaping from the connections is the delight of the sheathbills. These false doves are not to be trusted. They are actually very bold, taking over other birds' nests so that they can suck out the contents of the eggs and kill the chicks.

In the afternoon Chief Warrant Officer Le Lay ordered Corporal Neto to catch some rabbits so that he could make a stew. The corporal came back with three. One was still moving. He finished it off with a sharp blow from the edge of his hand. Neto has a thin face, piercing eyes, and the nose of a bird of prey. He is a man of few words.

After snaring the rabbits he went up the hill with his paraglider and began to fly over the ruins like a skua. Sometimes the wind took him up very high. He circled down again gently. From time to time he lets his body go limp like a hanged man, with his head lolling down towards the ground.

I'll never forget his calm, keen falcon's gaze as he looked at us. We applauded him. The enigmatic smile of the sphinx with the bird's wings didn't change. Then he suddenly sailed off again towards the sea. We were worried that he might be blown towards Long Island, but he came back, swooping down on us. Then he landed near the shore. The long wings of his parachute fell about him. He pushed them away.

His long, hard hands looked like talons.

2

When will the *Aventure* come back?

The days fly by at Port Jeanne d'Arc. They are so intangible that the paras can't manage to fix them in a strict chronology. Is it Monday or Tuesday? Time has become a matter for dispute.

One evening the radio picks up the overseas service of Radio France. To us this voice from another world seems unnatural, like a parody. We listen to these well-organized but fragile words, which might be swallowed up at any moment by the next station on the band. The subject is the Gulf War, the uprising in the holy towns of Karbala and Nayef. Then an expert begins to speak. He uses the current expressions:

"I only want to prove," "that's the reason why," and begins all his sentences with "I'd like to point out." Why do these words sound so hollow and insincere to me? These words from so far away should have seemed friendly. Why does their lack of substance shock me? This man is not saying anything, not thinking anything. He has an answer for everything. The journalist interviewing him annoys me too. He keeps saying, "Right. In concrete terms, what's going to happen?"

I long for someone to ask him, "In abstract terms, what's going to happen?" It's a disconcerting question that could perhaps elicit more than these so-called concrete terms that just cloud reality. Besides, the word *concrete* refers to something substantial, thick, heavy, pasty. When you are wading through the Kerguelen bogs, this is something concrete. Nevertheless, Kerguelen itself is not concrete. It escapes reality and is subject only to the imagination.

The concrete, this illusion of getting into "the heart of the matter," is an invention of the devil. It reduces everything to the real, the actual, and to that alone. I'm thinking of Christ's temptation in the desert. Satan says to him, "In concrete terms, if you are the Son of God, turn these stones into bread."

Christ replies that man cannot live only by what is actual, "but by the word of God." Christ definitely says, "by the word," that is by words that transform things.

There's a modest little cemetery half hidden in the tufts of acaena on the hill overlooking Port Jeanne d'Arc. Three white crosses leaning in the same direction still hold out against the wind. A fourth has broken off. The stones that held it in the ground have nearly all been scattered. Only a small piece of wood remains held in place at the base by two stones.

These graves are one of the rare traces of mankind on Desolation Island, a treeless land that death has replanted with these memorials set on open, wind-swept ground. They are intermediaries between the brooding underworld and the bounding ether.

Captain Couesnon and I have decided to restore the fourth cross, picking up bits of wood with peeling paint lying here and there in the cemetery, probably from other, now untraceable, graves. They belong to Kaffirs and Zulus, the "Cape Boys" the Norwegians used to employ as laborers. On one cross, you can still make out some numbers: 1896–193... On another, the first name Karl and the ending of a word... ansen, obviously a Norwegian family name.

We bring back the pieces of wood so that we can make something out of them. In what seems like a few seconds, Corporal Neto has unearthed a rusty saw in the ruins and built a cross. When he has finished he brandishes it like an exorcist. I thank him, looking a little uneasy.

Captain Couesnon precedes me carrying the cross on his shoulder. The ascent of the calvary cross: the wind plays his balance as he climbs the hill. I go off to look for some large stones while my companion digs a hole to secure the base of the cross. How many years will it stay standing?

There used to be a huge crucifix on the site of Port Jeanne d'Arc. It was erected in 1924 but is no longer there. I suggest we go look for it. As we walk, the captain tells me the story of the man who put it there: Étienne Peau, assistant curator of the Natural History Museum of Le Havre.

Peau had made the journey as a cure for his delicate son's poor health. He stayed for a while at Port Jeanne d'Arc, which had resumed some of its former activities in 1920. Étienne Peau's son came back from Kerguelen strong and well again. Did the father put up the votive cross to thank heaven? In the monograph he wrote on his return, Étienne Peau rightly emphasizes the archipelago's invigorating climate. He stresses the fact that it gives health and strength as well as a great increase in appetite. The keenness and purifying clarity of the air are like the smell of the high peaks: fresh, lively, and with that slightly acid overtone typical of Kerguelen.

Sir John Nares, captain of the *Challenger*, a scientific vessel that came to observe the Transit of Venus in 1874, notes that "Kerguelen Island is very healthy; the only complaint is of being too hungry." Aubert de la Rüe confirms his opionion: "The air is pure and fresh, free from infectious germs. [. . .] Colds are almost unknown there." He also points out that the archipelago has no mosquitoes, the bane of northern regions.

Tramping over some clumps of acaena on the heights, we discover a mound of stones surrounded by a border marked out with pieces of brick. Could this be the place where the cross once stood?

Étienne Peau had put a message in a bottle to the effect that the monument was placed in the care of those who came to Kerguelen after him. I picture this enormous cross on the hill against Desolation's stormy sky.

Étienne Peau was poor and it was difficult for him get together the money he needed for the expedition. He took advantage of a steamship tanker, the *Oural*, which was taking coal and other merchandise to Kerguelen and bringing back oil from a prospective sea-elephant hunt. Once there, Peau was horrified by the huge slaughter of the marine animals. On his return, he lodged a protest with the French authorities. His report is the basis for the 30 December 1924 decree proclaiming certain parts of the archipelago's coast a protected national park.

Peau was a serious, determined man, yet he too succumbed to the illusions Kerguelen had so often inspired. At the end of his very careful report, he actually writes, "this land can perfectly well be colonized by families, who will find well-being, affluence, and prosperity in the midst of an abundance (of meat, eggs, etc.) unknown elsewhere, and made complete by the additional cultivation of a few European crops, various vegetables and potatoes." This idyllic picture does not match reality. There was an attempt at colonization by a few families at Port Couvreux four years later. It was a dismal failure. As for producing vegetables in the Kerguelens, so far no one has managed to do it, apart from growing them in a hothouse at Port aux Français.

Aubert de la Rüe speaks ironically of an article that appeared in the *Revue Economique Française* in 1932, suggesting that four hundred to five hundred people should be set up on Kerguelen in stock farms and villages, one of which would be at Port Jeanne d'Arc. The author foreshadowed the introduction of foxes to get rid of the rabbits and the arrival of Trappist monks. "This is a totally impractical idea," Aubert de la Rüe asserts, "completely in the spirit of Jean-Jacques Rousseau."

In 1982, the Réunion Socialist Party Federation thought of sending "a permanent settlement of people" there to help with unemployment in Réunion, pointing out that "the climate is no more difficult than in the Falklands."[2]

The sun has begun its descent behind the hills. A light reddish mist covers the islands in the distance. Close to the spot where we disembarked, a grave in good condition attracts our attention. The cross has a name, *Isak Steiner*, and a date, *1920*. Probably a Norwegian. A big, crimson flower is lying at the foot of the cross, a sort of washed-out red poppy. The flower has a strange feel when you touch it. It takes me a moment to realize that it's plastic. Who could have brought it here?

Who was Steiner? Did he have a family? Why is he buried

on the beach and not on the hill? Like busy grave diggers, we try to find some clue in the mound of stones and the cross with its pointed arms. The Bossière brothers signed a whaling contract in 1920 with a new Anglo-Norwegian firm, Irving and Johnson. It was allocated hunting rights for an area to the south of the island, as the shipowners from Le Havre kept the northern part for themselves.

Perhaps Isak Steiner was one of those who got Port Jeanne d'Arc going again at that time. You have the impression that he was buried on the shore in some haste. And yet the Norwegians didn't leave Port Jeanne d'Arc unexpectedly; it was as late as 1924 that they decided to abandon the station and treat the blubber directly on board factory ships. The Bossière brothers set up a fishing company with French capital to take up whaling themselves, but they could not halt the slow decline. Even though they used the equipment at Port Jeanne d'Arc, bought boats like the *Austral* or the *Espérance*, three years later Port Jeanne d'Arc was closed for good and Port Couvreux abandoned. For several years, there wasn't a living soul on Kerguelen.

Captain Couesnon is preparing a history of the Bossière brothers. I tell him about the religious service at Touffreville, where their graves are, and which he had a hand in setting up. He was actually the one who instigated the research to find René Bossière's burial vault. Learning that the concession for the plot had expired in 1979, he got in touch with the Rev. Father Bossière, who decided to repair the tomb and organize a ceremony at Touffreville in memory of his two uncles. The captain had written the speech, but he was not able to be present as he is based in Réunion.

"The Bossières weren't driven by any profit motive. It was more for the risk, the taste for adventure," the captain said.

Could they perhaps have wanted to be kings of Kerguelen? They used an official stamp with *"Résidence de France—Îles Kerguelen."* There are precedents for this. Last century, a man from Périgord, Antoine de Tounens, proclaimed himself king of Patagonia.

The Bossières wanted to create a kingdom, not royalty: a kingdom for France, not for themselves. The brothers' ambition was indeed to develop Kerguelen like Patagonia, where their father ran a factory rendering seal oil. The two brothers went there in 1881. They realized that Patagonia had many aspects in common with Kerguelen. They visited farms and saw sheep being raised. René Bossière even decided to spend five years in Argentina studying how to acclimatize sheep to Kerguelen. He also observed the English methods of raising sheep in the Falklands. In 1913 he bought a thousand sheep there destined for Port Couvreux. This flock was abandoned in 1914 because of the war. The Falkland sheep were old and bought cheaply. Many of them died during the journey.

"The Bossières often made unfortunate choices," the captain said. "Nevertheless, they worked all their lives to keep the Kerguelens French. The postal service has done them justice two years ago by issuing a stamp with their picture on it. The bronze plaque, which will be put in place in Port aux Français is a start in restoring them to favor.

The *Albatross*, which patrols the Kerguelens, brought back two alabaster urns containing Kerguelen soil to Touffreville, so that they could be placed in the tomb of the two brothers. Earth and the dead…

The captain stops in front of a marker that I took to be an ordinary cement post. It's a reminder of the voyage of the *Antarès*. You can make out the name and a date: 1931…

The letters are fading. In a few years there won't be any indication left of the visit of this dispatch vessel sent to Kerguelen by the French government to assert its sovereignty. This is a typically French way of doing things: send a war boat for a show of strength. And that's it; no follow-up at all. The *Bougainville* made the same tour of the archipelago in 1939. No Frenchman set foot on Kerguelen soil for the next ten years. They have to start from the very beginning every time.

While we are walking through the ruins, Corporal Neto swoops towards us hanging from his glider flapping his fallen archangel's wings. Might he not be the only man to have discovered the secret of the wind here? He makes use of it instinctively, riding every thermal. He hasn't tamed the wind, he has understood it, borne aloft by the miraculous bellows.

"He's the king of Kerguelen!"

He sails off towards the green meadows of sea tangle that spread along the coast, so thickly that the sheathbills patter over it as though it were solid ground.

The bird-man is floating in the gentle evening air that softens the outline of the volcanic hills in the distance. As he comes towards us, the ground at Port Jeanne d'Arc suddenly begins to glitter with thousands of little spear-shaped flashes of light. For the moment we stare in amazement at this marvel. But it has nothing to do with the sphinx looking down on us. All the pieces of glass normally invisible to the naked eye have suddenly lit up. These fragments from broken windows have become stuck in the ground in a myriad of tiny splinters. This glorious light blinds the big bird. It catches him by surprise and he hesitates. His wings begin to collapse. He has caught the dazzling flash beneath him and he lands clumsily, his eyes hurting.

It gave him quite a shock.

3

I'm still waiting for the *Aventure,* which is supposed to take me to Port aux Français. The paras, who are beginning their expedition, are due to leave Port Jeanne d'Arc this morning. I'll go with them for a few hours as far as Snow Valley.

A cat jumps out from behind a rock: a vision of a black head with a pointed gash of white from its eyes down towards its nose. The white stamp splits the upturned snout of a nose, making the head look monstrously shrunk. It's like a demon or an incubus spirit appearing in a flash of lightning.

A cat in the Kerguelens! There are actually thousands of them in the archipelago. They are feral animals, descendants of pets abandoned by sealers and men on winter missions. They have puzzled the scientists for quite a long time. Contrary to all expectation, when they returned to the wild their craniums shrank in size. Normally when domestic animals are abandoned and manage to survive, their cerebral capacity increases. They then realized that this great predator has no predator of its own to fear. On this treeless land, where birds build their nests on the ground, feral cats devour thousands of young petrels.[3] They also eat a lot of young rabbits. They have no rivals, so that no effort is required to get food. Hence their "intelligence" has regressed. They are very wary: about twenty years ago, the administration gave a liter of pastis for every ten cats caught.

We've come to a plateau strewn with stones, as though the ground had been bombed. The air the wind blows here is pure and bracing. As a matter of fact, the map shows that the place is called Wind Plateau.

I'm intrigued by rusty colored spots between the stones. They are shaped like little hemispherical mounds. It's *Azorella selago*, an umbelliferous plant that grows in such tight clumps it looks like moss. It's also pleasantly soft to the touch. These little velvet cushions delicately placed on the ground soften the harshness of the landscape.

Another plateau made of brownish sand appears in front of us. No sooner have I put my foot on the sandy surface, quite restful after the stones, than I sink into it right up to my midthigh. The ground is saturated with water not visible on the surface and it is imperceptibly pulling at me. The suction noise, like a sink emptying, makes me feel as though I'm being dragged down into mud that's becoming softer and softer. I plunge my fingers into the mud, trying to hold on, but I can't get a grip. Standing at the edge of the quivering sand, the captain is holding out his hand to me. When I got out of the thick, wet slime, I was covered with a grey, slightly greasy film, like a newborn baby smeared with sebum coming out of the amniotic fluid.

The presence of shifting sands on the hilltop comes from the slow destruction of rocks carried along by rain and thawing snow. The particles, which look firm and dry, form a basin and build up on the surface. The solid appearance of the ground is all the more deceptive because the pool of water is not visible on the surface. I read in the account written by John Nunn, the Robinson Crusoe of Kerguelen, that one of his companions nearly perished in this ooze when he was out duck hunting. In 1922, two employees of the whaling station never returned after venturing out separately into this part of the archipelago. All efforts to find them were unsuccessful.

A dense fog is coming towards us, getting thicker as it approaches. It soon envelops us and we can't see any farther than a few yards. The light is as dim as at dusk. The captain gives the order to stop behind some large rocks. The drizzle stings like fine hail. We can hear the whispering sound as it trickles between the rocks, which have streaks of foamy water running down them. When the wind blows in the silence of the high country, its voice is choked and sorrowful. Its breath is short and comes in a series of stifled contractions.

The eight soldiers are walking on ahead of me. Their oilskins make their bodies and especially their heads look rounder, as though they were astronauts wandering between jets of steam on an unknown planet. Captain Couesnon has stopped to point out a Kerguelen cabbage with the stick he is carrying. With its heads of leaves packed very tightly together at the heart, this plant looks something like a corn stalk. This cabbage really appeals to me. In French we say "stupid as a cabbage," but the Kerguelen cabbage is not stupid at all. No one knows where it came from, probably from a time when the weather was very hot, which should have meant it wouldn't survive later. But it has survived, adapting to the climatic conditions of the archipelago. Its leaves contain ascorbic acid, the best cure for scurvy. Without this *Pringlea antiscorbuta*, which has nothing to do with our good old European cabbage with its big coarse leaves, many a sailor would have died. It has been chosen to symbolize Kerguelen on the coat of arms of the Southern Lands. It's the mandrake, the miracle plant of the Desolation Islands, the proof than you can find something useful in anything, even in a desperate situation.

I taste one of its leaves, to show my respect. It's tart, even very peppery. I like the rhizome better: it has a pleasant bitterness, something like radish or horseradish. It seems that this cabbage is excellent as a salad, but it mustn't be cooked in water. I read in an account from the fifties that it then gives off "a musky odor, strangely reminiscent of the smell of the least virtuous girls in the Algerian Casbah."

The absence of trees and the presence of fog explain why noises sound so strange here. There is not the slightest rustle on this bare plateau, nothing but voices. Is it the wind or my companions? The invisible voices murmur above me like the spirits of the air. I can make out a dark shape. It's Captain Couesnon waving his stick at me. He looks like the archangel brandishing the flaming sword at the outcasts of the Garden of Eden.

The landscape still seems to bear traces of the world when it had just come into being and was still unfinished. Creation stopped at the fifth day with the birds and the fishes. Perhaps Kerguelen sensed this cursed aspect of the land. This impatient Breton dreamer from the land of the mysterious Armorican mists was, after all, closer to Ossian than the Enlightenment. Unlike Bougainville, he was not a part of the learned and philosophical society of his time. He was a man on his own; he knew solitude and *desolation*. These islands were always meant for him.

I've always wanted to know where he came from, know the country where he spent his childhood. The manor house where he was born is a few miles from Quimper, in the heart of the *glaʒik* country.[4] It has scarcely changed since Yves-Joseph de Kerguelen was born there in 1734. The Château de Trémarec is a traditional small Breton manor house with its hexagonal tower, crossbar windows, and the noble simplicity of granite and slate. Kerguelen, the holly house (*Ker Kelenn*), is the inspiration for this noble family's motto: "Ever green" (*"Vert en tout temps"*). There is nothing martial in this phrase, but it is still there today on the coat of arms of the Kerguelen Islands. "Ever green," but also as prickly as the holly leaf and these drops of rain stinging my face.

What a shock it must have been for this well-born Breton who set out to discover "Gonneville Land." The legendary continent that had obsessed navigators for two and a half centuries was nothing but a vast ruin.

The king's instructions to Kerguelen were quite clear: "There is every indication that a very large continent exists to the south of the Saint Paul and Amsterdam Islands and it should occupy a part of the globe extending from 45 degrees of latitude south down to the regions of the pole, in an immense area as yet unexplored. It does, however, appear reasonably well-established that Monsieur Gonneville landed there in about 1504 and stayed there for almost six months...." We know today that Gonneville's mysterious land was the coast of Brazil.

We start to feel for Kerguelen when he comes back from his first voyage and pretends to be enthusiastic: "It is a fifth part of the world and the land I have named France in the Southern Sea (*la France australe*) is so situated that it could hold sway over India, the Moluccas, China, and the Southern Sea." He has ensnared himself in the idea of his "Australasia." In a report, he suggests sending fifty families "of poor Acadians who are living today in the most dire poverty in various corners of France."[5] Kerguelen, the castaway of his own discovery!

Why did he come to the ends of the earth to discover its secret? It may be hidden in his Château de Trémarec.

Kerguelen wrote a great deal, and not only to justify himself. He inundated the Ministry of the Navy with memoranda on how to wage war on England, which actually contained some pertinent suggestions, or on some detail about fitting out ships. He even submitted a model capstan to his superiors. Many of his writings have not yet been studied and lie there in his manor house, which still belongs to his family. I'm convinced that the explanation of his behavior is in those unpublished archives.

The court-martial, which handed down its verdict on 15 May 1775, declared him "duly charged and convicted of nine offenses of various degrees of seriousness."

Kerguelen had committed "nine offenses." He was guilty of having "illicitly and secretly taken a girl on board" and "living scandalously" with his female passengers; "of having taken on board various commercial goods and sold them privately on commission or on his own behalf"; of having slept on land at the Cape; of "not ensuring that the justice and order prescribed by His Majesty's ordinances were observed on his ship"; "of having compromised his authority in various instances"; "of having acted badly when a mast was lost during a storm"; "of having not followed instructions by failing to search for Nategat Island"; "of having made each of his officers individually sign a declaration in which he declared he was abandoning his exploration"; and finally "of having drawn up a libelous report and submitted it to the trial."

For all of these acts, Kerguelen was cashiered and "from that day excluded from the officer corps of the Navy," declared "unable to ever serve the King in his Navy, to have forfeited and been stripped of all honors and prerogatives of that corps." And finally he was sentenced to six years in prison.

On 30 May 1775, at three o'clock in the morning, the chevalier de Kerguelen was awoken in his cell and taken to the Château de Saumur. He was detained there for three years. During the course of the preliminary investigation of the case, Kerguelen's handwriting becomes more and more illegible. The real question remains: was he the victim of a plot? I've thought for some time that the investigation was not carried out impartially. I'm less sure today. And yet it's clear that he was unjustly convicted. It's no less clear that the questioning, the hearing of the witnesses, the confrontations with the accused, the commissioners' very detailed inquiry were on the whole according to law. Moreover, Kerguelen objected so little to the procedure that he consequently entreated his judges to print it "in its entirety," at his own expense, so that public opinion could judge "impartially."

It must be admitted that Kerguelen often put himself in the wrong, but most of his "offenses" are nothing more than peccadilloes, when they are examined one by one. The misfortune is having let them accumulate. So many violations of the rules—it's a lot for one man. Having Louison on board was illegal but common practice at that time. Unfortunately for Kerguelen, her presence unleashed the young officers' hostility against him. He set a bad example. Being in a vulnerable position, Kerguelen could not react against the climate of conspiracy and intrigue. And when he did decide to reprimand a member of his crew, he did it in quite the wrong way, publicly insulting an officer who set himself up as a rival.

"He had to watch Louison's conduct. She was attached to him more out of self-interest than affection," one of his accusers testifies. While he defends himself nearly always convincingly on the eight other matters, he remains strangely silent when it comes to Louise Sequin. "It is a misdemeanor in which I had given my word," he said.

Part of the mystery about Kerguelen is contained in that phrase. What does he mean? He had given his word. Put another way, he is bound by a promise or an oath. But what has he promised? To whom? He won't say anything more about it. Facing his judges, he gives only the following detail: "A pension of 300 pounds, which I pay her in a convent, will remind me of it all my life." What is this debt he owes to Louison? When they put in at Réunion before leaving for the Desolations, he nonetheless tried to get rid of her while they were in port.

His only serious misdeed is no doubt having been negligent in preparing for his second voyage. Why had he given up before he had even left? He agreed to sail in a brand new ship, the *Roland*. The wood used in the hull was too green and sappy. The holds were damp. The provisions putrefied, as they were stored at the bottom of the boat. When it got to Desolation Island, the food was eaten by maggots. This disaster was one of the main reasons for his hasty return to Madagascar. "Why did Kerguelen, who was an expert sailor and intrepid explorer, act in such a feeble way on this second expedition?" Roger Vercel wonders.[6]

The discoverer of France in the southern sea was unlucky. Released by the king, he didn't serve out the whole of his sentence and was able to go to sea again. However, he was not allowed to rejoin the "Grand Corps." And so Kerguelen became a privateer. Bad luck pursued him. Stopped and inspected by the British, he was thrown into prison a second time. He lost almost everything: his ship, which had cost him a great deal to fit out, and above all a chance for revenge on the court of Versailles.

Lastly, Kerguelen was not a man who could change easily; he was not *flexible*, as we say of someone who is a schemer and good at adapting to the prevailing circumstances. He withdrew to his Château de Trémarec and used his enforced leisure to describe his voyages to the South Lands and proclaim his innocence. He wanted to let people know his version of the affair and to answer Pagès, who had already published his account of the voyage.

The Account of Two Voyages in the Southern Seas and India, published in Paris by Knapen is a work highly valued by bibliophiles today. It received the king's authorization to publish in 1782 and raised the ire of his former colleagues and his judges. The Keeper of the Seals prohibited its sale and pulped it in the following year, but the order was not carried out very strictly, as the book can be found in nearly all the rare book collections of the major libraries.

One sentence at the end of the work has always intrigued me: "The time to justify myself has not yet arrived, but this justification will appear, at a happier time for me or after my death."

4

The mist allows a few yellow rays of light to filter through, turning it a light coffee color. The paras loom up ahead of us. Their raincoats look brand new, as though the surface has been slowly flaking off, leaving slowly fading patches of fog behind them. Suddenly, the sky becomes clear. The young leader of the paras looks at his map. A real camaraderie has grown up between him and Captain Couesnon, who is standing a little to one side. In any case, he's not in a parachute division, but in transport.

I admire his skill at finding our position on the map. We are very close to Snow Valley, to the northwest of the Jeanne d'Arc Peninsula. The water in the fast-flowing river is transparent and gushes out in the midst of enormous rocks. I leave my companions at the river bank, while they continue on their way towards the south. I feel rather sad as I watch them disappear behind a hill. Captain Couesnon gives me a last wave. He was a good companion.

I'm going back to Port Jeanne d'Arc alone for one last night. Tomorrow morning, the lighter *Aventure* should come to pick me up, weather permitting, and take me back to Port aux Français.

Striding over the open land covered with acaena, I'm suprised for the first time by a quivering between the clumps followed by a mad scamper of something I can't identify straight away. The acaena stems grow to at least twenty inches high. There's a second, sudden rustling and, between two dry, woody roots, I can see a rabbit dashing off like lightning through the leaves. A whole network of galleries branches out under my feet. The ground is riddled with hundreds of burrows, which slowly undermine the acaena roots. The wind eventually tears them up, leaving holes in the carpet of plants and revealing the rabbits' underground hideouts. They have wiped out not only the cabbage from Grande Terre (the main island), but also the azorella, as its base is eaten away by the burrows.

The rabbits dart off this way and that under my feet. Sometimes the wind sends great shadows running across the acaena. Strangely enough, it's not passing clouds that create these wide dark patches on the open land, but the slightly concave shape of the leaves themselves. The outside is shiny, while the inside is dull. The fields of acaena move in waves like a sea swell as the changing wind either bends or lifts them.

Now and again I trip, either catching my feet in the roots or falling right over because of an unexpected rabbit hole opened up by the wind. But in this grassy plain, to me it's a pleasurable sensation. The grass comes up to my waist and gives off that nice, sharp smell mixed with overtones of wet, heavy earth. I listen to the invisible spirit of the wind; it bores into the southern ocean lucern as it does into the wheat just before harvest time. I feel free. There are no paths in Kerguelen, no tracks made by feet continually passing over the same land. Nothing is signposted. Notices spoil places.

A sign in front of rows of vines has to indicate "vineyard," or beside large stretches of pines south of Bordeaux, "Landais Pine Forest." If the freeway passes any sort of rise, there is a notice announcing "Hill," as if people couldn't identify a river, a church, or a castle.

Kerguelen has escaped this danger. A host of names have been stuck on a map, but they don't mean much. With its Joffre or Foch peninsulas, its Marne or Clemenceau bays, Desolation Island tries to be a corner of France like any others. Yet Kerguelen is hardly French at all. It's neither human nor inhuman: it's a-human. I can't find any other words than *open plains* or *meadows* for these stretches of acaena, as green as any lawn, but they are not covered with grass. And the wind is completely different from cyclones, tornadoes, or typhoons, those rather common furies. It blows in a crescendo; it growls in a voice from another world. Even at its worst, it still sings, vibrating like a column of air in a huge pipe.

The seagulls and petrels never manage to drown the sound of the organ bellows. It's easy to imagine they are applauding or berating you. Inexhaustible nature gives generously of herself to whomever asks her. In Kerguelen, the strong draw energy, the weak become exhausted, the dreamers become entrenched in their illusions. Everything people bring with them increases too quickly: rabbits, dreams...

I remember how I felt in the eighties, when the press reported neutron bomb tests in Kerguelen. The information was false. But someone must have imagined that this remote, virgin, and uninhabited land could be put to good use. It's rumored that when activities at the nuclear base at Mururoa cease, trials will take place in the Kerguelens. For the moment they are only rumors, however, at the end of the Algerian War, when the installations in the Sahara had to be relinquished, it was proposed to General de Gaulle that nuclear tests should be carried out in the Kerguelens. The army dissuaded him, preferring lagoons in the Pacific. At any rate, according to the scientists, the geology of the archipelago is admirably suited to underground explosions.

The misfortune for Kerguelen is that it "lends itself" to far too many things. Rockets were already launched there in the seventies.[7] Geophysicists have built an ultramodern station out of Port aux Français. They praise the untouched nature of this part of the world, far from electromagnetic disturbances connected with the presence of humans, free from all pollution that could affect measurements. Yves de Kerguelen himself extolled the advantages his discovery offered to science: "A remote continent, which has never communicated with the others, and which is a world apart, should provide enlightening clarification about the upheavals that have occurred in the world."

With the center of the Antarctic and a few mid-Pacific arch-ipelagos, Kerguelen is one of the three privileged places on our planet. The effects of human presence on the composition of the atmosphere are felt least in those places. Kerguelen is also an ideal spot for orbitographic beacons that help Argos and Sarsat satellites to take their bearings. The equipment installed by the National Center for Space Studies (CNES) will soon enable data from the Helios and Spot 4 satellites to be gathered and transmitted to Toulouse through the INTELSAT system.

All these impending threats spoil my pleasure. One day these beautifully colored pebbles will be covered with plastic drums and dirty paper covered in greasy fuel oil.

When I arrive back at the ruins of Port Jeanne d'Arc, it's almost night. Near the broken-down wharf, I notice several shadowy shapes, which immediately disappear behind the rusty barrels. As I move closer, I can hear little grunting noises. It's a group of penguins. There are about ten of them and they don't seem too afraid of my presence. I'm surprised by their size: their height must be at least three feet. They stand up very straight with their white aprons across their stomachs and that rather stiff, mocking look of a waiter taking a rise out of the maître d'hôtel.

The house is empty. During the night, the wind started up its infernal dance. The ghostly mouth whispered sighs and songs that sounded like laments into my ear. I thought of the Kaffirs buried on the hill, of Isak Steiner, imploring ghosts, shivering in their loneliness.

I'm woken up in the middle of the night by knocking that shakes the walls. I light the lamp. The flame whispers incomprehensibly, sending out sizzling sparks that sound like words said aloud. Draughts reduce it to a tiny blue point of acetylene then it flares up again a moment later.

I feel desolate and alone. Is this the hour of my real meeting with Kerguelen? The island has created a vacuum around me to bring about this encounter in the depths of the Port Jeanne d'Arc night. Might not the howls and the ghosts simply be a diversion, setting the scene for a confession? Desolation's ghosts have come to question me tonight. I can feel their presence and their slightly sour breath in my face. What was my purpose in coming here? I cite my childhood dream and become aware of a disturbing, aggrieved silence, as if my answer was pathetic and I would have to bring out my major defenses. I cite the tragedy of isolation, which is Yves de Kerguelen's tragedy. He had to face up alone to the disappointment of discovery, the fraud of France in the southern seas, the hostility of his officers, the dishonor of his trial and conviction. Desolation had always belonged to him. He went towards his mirror and drew back at the last minute, terrified by what he saw. He would be forced to look again at what frightened him. To look back is to lose everything.

My inner voice tells me I must stop hiding behind Yves de Kerguelen. "I came here to grieve, to be alone, to bring new life into what has been destroyed."

Outside, the rain is lashing down. The storm hits the hut with enough force to uproot it. The gutterless roof cannot get rid of the rainwater, which pours down and surges spasmodically like breath about to choke. The house is carried on the water. It has cut its moorings to the world of the living.

"Noah built the ark in which few were saved through water." (First Epistle of Peter)

5

The weather is overcast, the sea stormy. I've been watching for the supply boat since dawn. The wind has become stronger and stronger, and has probably prevented the *Aventure* from setting out from port. I'll have to spend an extra day at Port Jeanne d'Arc, perhaps more. Will I ever get to see my arch?

I've just heard a kind of squealing, a short, shrill, repeated cry I momentarily took to be an animal. Something has suddenly emerged from the slate grey sea near Long Island. I can tell it's the barge from its squat shape banging against the waves. Paulo, the quartermaster, has been signaling me from the bridge by sounding the siren as a note of welcome. The *Aventure*'s first mate is a taciturn Tahitian. His large hand gets a firm grip on the passenger and hauls him on to the deck.

Bad news. Before going back to Port aux Français, the *Aventure* has to go to High Island then down again to Cemetery Island. To help me be patient, the quartermaster suggests setting me down for a few hours in Observatory Bay so that I can look at the site of a camp set up by Germans at the beginning of the century.

There are wild sheep on High Island, introduced into the Kerguelen Islands in 1957. Paulo says that they have become well adapted to a climate that is very different from their native Corsica. After destroying the Kerguelen cabbage, they are now threatening the azorella.

"The ground on High Island is completely cropped. It's like a lunar landscape," Paulo informs me, maneuvering his boat with extraordinary skill through a labyrinth of channels and reefs. The bays all have the same tabular outline, descending down to the sea in steps. Huge rock falls are piled up at the foot of crenellated walls and amphitheaters with crumbling stairs.

Huge numbers of birds fly off as we approach, their wings beating slowly and silently. There is a tang in the air; the sky is full of the lens-shaped clouds, typical of the Kerguelens. They are piled up like plates and can stay like that for hours, in spite of the wind.

Observatory Bay has just come into view. I've only a few hours to look over the place.

"I hope to call back for you in a while. Weather permitting," jokes the quartermaster, slapping a packet of biscuits into my hand. As I jump out, I see that he's not really joking. Do you give provisions to someone who is only staying for a few hours? Aren't biscuits survival rations for sailors? Paulo has also had the amusing idea of putting me ashore at the foot of a grave. And a very beautiful one at that, the most artistic I've seen in Kerguelen.

The cross has sculptured motifs and bears an inscription indicating that it is the grave of a sailor from the *Volage*, who died on 14 December 1874, aged twenty-three. The name has disappeared. The wood in the cross, worn by the wind and rain, is remarkably smooth and shiny. Before the Germans, there was an English scientific mission landed here by the *Volage* for a three-month stay to observe the transit of Venus.

Venus or "the shepherd's star" is the brightest in the night sky, after the moon. There was no other place on earth as good as Kerguelen for watching it cross the sun. In 1874 there were at least ten ships in the archipelago, without counting the whalers. The Germans had sent a warship, the *Arcona*, and especially the *Gazelle*, which took very precise hydrographic readings on the northeast coast. The German raiders that came in 1940 to shelter in the Kerguelens while they changed the camouflage of their ships used the maps drawn sixty-six years earlier by the *Gazelle* expedition.

Germany, a country of geographers, was enthusiastic about Kerguelen well before France. The *Valdivia* spent time there on its way back from the Antarctic in 1898. What were the Germans looking for on Kerguelen? Certainly the same thing as I: the revelation of a hidden truth! Apart from the fact that theirs was scientific. They patiently examined the archipelago and were well aware of its disturbing paradox. It comes out in all their observations. Karl Chun, leader of the *Valdivia* expedition, has no hesitation in writing, for example, that the Kerguelens were revealed to him "in Heavenly splendor." Fascinated by the "romance" of Christmas Harbor, he constantly wonders about this strange country. When was it formed? Why is it so green?

Karl Chun's questions no doubt formed the basis of the 1902 mission. This time the Germans decided to study the archipelago thoroughly and set up a mission there for a year. It was the first winter scientific mission in the history of Kerguelen. Two ships left the botanist Emile Werth, the geographer Karl Luyken, Dr. Josef Enzenperger, and two domestic staff, Urbanski and Wienke, at Observatory Bay. There were also some Chinese coolies. The mission was set up on the site of the 1874 English astronomical mission.

It's raining as I go searching for some trace of the camp. After having wandered about for nearly an hour, I finally catch sight of a stone placed on the ground. It doesn't look as though it comes from Kerguelen. It's white, cut in the shape of a cube and bears an inscription: "MW 15W." I figure that this perfectly proportioned meteorite set in the midst of a jumble of rocks represents the enigma of Kerguelen: the stone chest, the double of the other arch. The rectangle is fixed to the ground as though waiting for something. It's a foundation. To receive what?

Not far from the platform with the sibylline inscription, I discover the ruins of the camp in the shelter of a hill. All that is left are roof-tree and framework, two baskets and two rolls of linoleum. It's nothing like Port Jeanne d'Arc, with a huge, endless jumble spread around the original site. Here, there is just a miserable, shapeless little cave-in, a powdery residue looking more like a heap of ashes than ruins. Only one vestige of human habitation, monumentally incongruous, attracts attention: a large stack of empty bottles; pot-bellied bottles with long necks, superb, conical, hand-blown Bordeaux bottles, heavy ringed Burgundy bottles, which would be the delight of any collector. Some are filled with water. Having read Enzenperger's diary, I know that the three Germans were hard drinkers. What else was there to do in a hole like this?

At the beginning of his account, Enzenperger good-humoredly describes their work and how they spend their time: building the library, going on trips with the dogs, making the routine collection of meteorological and magnetic data. Then one day, something tragic happens. The German scientist notices that his legs are swollen. He immediately thinks of beriberi, an illness caused by a lack of Vitamin B. Two coolies have already died. Instead of giving way to despair, he contemplates his death quite stoically. He is more sorry for his two companions, who are also affected by the illness.

This cold, factual description of the sickness, told by a man who knows he will never see his homeland again, is deeply moving. In this confined space face to face with death, he never complains. He keeps on working, seeing to his dogs, keeping up his diary so that people will understand, as he puts it, "what happened." The edema spreads throughout his body. He is pleased when he finally finds a horizontal position that stops all his limbs from becoming filled with water. That is the last sentence in the diary. A note has been added, indicating the exact spot where Enzenperger was buried.

As I stand there alone in the middle of the abandoned camp, I can't take my eyes off the remains of a bunk bed, where Enzenperger may have died. The rain slides down the tubular metal frame and falls in heavy drops on the linoleum, which flaps with irritating regularity. I soon have to take shelter behind the hill, because the rain is falling much more heavily before a violent wind. I stay huddled in my little retreat but at least I'm protected from the storm. To help pass the time, I leaf through Rallier du Baty and my Delépine, which informs me of a curious fact about Enzenperger's journal. Nothing happened to it for a long time, then it was finally published in 1924. Later on, this book was to figure prominently in the library of the famous Nazi *Ordenburgen* for the "moral" edification of young Germans.[8]

Rallier gives his impressions of coming across the ruins of this camp quite by chance with Eugène Larose, one of the three sailors from the *J.-B.-Charcot*: "There was something strange and disturbing about this abandoned house." Rallier comments: "The dark windows look out like empty eyes in hollow sockets." Once inside the house, he notices that it had been abandoned hurriedly "as if the occupants had been disturbed in their routine by the warning of some attack, fleeing without taking the time to bring anything with them. The saucepans, dishes, and plates were there, exactly as if the inhabitants of the house had been surprised sitting at the table, eating their last meal. But, for some unknown reason, the meal had not been touched. The cast-iron cook pots still contained a kind of stew covered with a thick layer of mold and riddled with a host of bacilli."

This section on Observatory Bay is bizarre and alarming, with more than a hint of Edgar Allen Poe weirdness. Nothing is as it should be, as in this scene where Rallier discovers the clothes hanging on a coat stand. "When the twilight shadows crept into the cabin, these clothes took on human form, looking for all the world like bodies hanging on hooks." But the most disturbing part concerns a night when he was alone, just a few yards away from the rock where I am now!

"I was preparing my evening meal, my hands busy with whatever utensils I needed. Dusk had fallen on the cabin and outside an oppressive silence reigned, that strange time when the day birds settle down for the night and the night birds have not yet woken up. I was humming a little song when I thought I heard a slight sound, as if someone was moving about out there. I think that when you live alone, your senses are more acute, something like those of a wild animal. I kept quiet with my hand in the air holding a plate or some such thing, and I listened carefully, like an animal surprised in its lair. But I was as completely alone as a man could be. I started working again and once more I froze and a sensation of fear—fear of the unknown—overcame me in spite of myself. There certainly was something moving, very furtively, in front of my door.

"Once again I dismissed the idea, trying to regain control of my wild imagination. Then, for some reason, my attention was drawn towards the window with its broken panes. I felt the most horrible sensation. Someone was there looking at me!

"Two astonished eyes in a wan face were staring straight at me. This frightening pale face was observing me with some curiosity. Then it disappeared and once again I heard the furtive noise that had attracted my attention. I stood there petrified, hardly able to breathe, almost choking. And once more I had to struggle with myself.

"It wasn't possible! It must have been a play of light or perhaps my senses were playing tricks on me. Perhaps I was going mad. Perhaps these long days on my own had been too much for me. I stood still, forcing myself to laugh to dispel this stupid fear. And then—once again—the white face appeared at the window, that ghostly head and the staring eyes with the yellow gleam in them.

"I picked up something—I don't know what—and with a strangled cry rushed to the door. I had to at least see the thing clearly before I went completely mad. As I leapt through the doorway with my weapon raised, I saw a white shape disappearing into the darkness. It was the shape of an animal, even though I had never heard of any animal on Desolation Island, apart from sea elephants and whales. As I rushed after it, the white shape bounded forward and found itself in the open. It was a dog! A husky with white fur, fat and obviously well fed. I was as startled as if it had been a real ghost, for it was surprising to say the least to find a dog on Desolation Island. During the two or three days that followed, he kept within call of the Germans' cabin, watching everything I did and taking a great interest in it.

"I tried to gain his confidence time and time again. I would walk towards him slowly, talking to him affectionately. 'Doggy! Good dog! Here, doggy!' But when I got to within about twenty paces of him, he ran off, and nothing I did could ever persuade him to be friendly. The dog followed us everywhere during the whole of our stay on this part of the island, but always at a distance, and we saw him miles away from the Germans' house. He lived in Elizabeth Bay, hunting the rabbits that were numerous on Kerguelen, and seemed to be the last of his pack."

Even though I tell myself that Rallier just had a fright, I can't deny that there is an inexplicable and terrifying sense of possible danger in these ruins. It's five o'clock and the *Aventure* still hasn't returned. Land and sea merge in the same sudden grey chill. Where will I spend the night if the *Aventure* doesn't come? I thought I had the weather on my side, but now I realize that its almost excessive kindness was nothing but a trick to keep me away from the black arch. To keep my spirits up, I try to think of all the nights that Rallier must have spent in the open. He was shivering with cold, but never complained.

I grope my way out of my shelter to be in full view at the same spot where I landed. When I look in front of me, all I can see is the poor sailor's cross. Its broken right arm looks like an amputated stump. The rigid cross, the silence, the mist, the concealed rocks, the silver tears falling... The heavy pall of the land of the dead suddenly descends on me. I can't help think of Enzenperger's companion, Werth, who also nearly died. The third man, Luyken, wasn't very able-bodied either. Like me, they watched and waited for the boat. On 30 March 1903, the survivors heard a steamship whistle. It was the *Stassfurt*. Werth, who was dying, was carefully winched aboard. Everything was left where it was, which explains Rallier du Baty's surprise when he entered the abandoned house five years later.

Preoccupied with the unfortunate end of the German mission, I haven't really been paying attention to a kind of panting noise that pulsates and then dies down. What I took to be the sound of the surf is the soft throb of an engine. The supply boat looms up in front of me.

With a mocking look on his face, and resignedly extending an open hand towards me to show solidarity with his temperamental boat, Paulo shouts in my direction, "I nearly forgot you. When the mist fell, I remembered you were there. You see, I faced every danger to come and fetch you." His expression became anxious when his caught the eye of his first mate, the Tahitian. His voice changed.

"We'll have to be cautious. We'll go back to the anchorage at High Island, where we were earlier. That's where we'll spend the night."

Another delay! I think of John Nunn's companions roaming Desolation Island for two years. They race along the coast of the archipelago to search the horizon. There's an excellent word in the French language to describe the power to endure: *longanimité*, which literally means being long-winded (*long-animité*). They have been running even faster since they discovered the sea elephant with the mysterious spear wound. They stop, out of breath, to look at a huge albatross, flying back and forth over the rocks. The shipwrecked men are fascinated by its flight. Suddenly one of the exclaims, "God bless my soul, John, it's the peak of a cutter."

Still panting, they go down to the shore. The Union Jack has been raised to the top of a mast to let them know they have been sighted.

The engine is running very slowly. Leaning over the front of the boat with his head nearly touching the water, the Tahitian is lowering and raising his arms. Paulo immediately interprets this semaphore learned from being repeated so often. The boat moves forward so gently that it seems to be sounding the waters. We almost touch a wall of rock; the boat proceeds steadily along it; the black water gurgles between the rock and the hull. The engine sputters so slowly as it sucks in water that you take it for the sound of cormorants diving. Paulo thinks the wall is Mussel Island.

The mist disappears over the gulf just as quickly as it fell. It divides into thin sheets that flutter in the air like butterflies before melting away in a few brief rays of sunlight. They absorb the wisps of smoke without leaving any trace behind, suddenly revealing a bare, glazed land, with whole slabs torn out like a mining landscape. It's High Island, home of the wild sheep. They have cropped all the vegetation. Halfway up a hill in the distance, I can see a slight trembling of the stripped ground. These almost invisible grey spots are all shaking in the same direction.

"The wild sheep!" the Tahitian shouts. There are about twenty in single file balancing on a rock face that falls sheer into the sea. The Tahitian has already got out on land and disappears behind the rocks. Corsican sheep in Kerguelen! How did they get here? One more mystery. The few existing documents, which I've consulted, are not clear on the subject. A report from 1961 hints that their introduction was one of the results of "the impression of isolation." Yet sheep are not companion animals. The ovines struggle to survive: they are reduced to eating seaweed and many die in winter.

The bay where we are moored is protected from the west wind. The Tahitian has returned, carrying a bundle. He gives us a strange smile and carefully begins to open up the cloth. He has an armful of mushrooms, pinkish with downy tops. Hardly believing my eyes, I run my fingers over their damp, silky flesh, which has a fresh smell of yeast and anise. He has prepared a fricassee on the stove and mixes it with some rice. The dish is enhanced by the taste and consistency of the mushrooms delicately seasoned with an unknown spice.

The weather has cleared up again. The first stars seem to

touch the top of the island. The wind has risen and growls all night. Dull thuds pass along the boat and echo because of the wooden deck. Sometimes the wind stops suddenly, and there is the heart of silence, in the infinite shimmering night.

The silence of Kerguelen is an interlude rather than an absence of noise. Without the contrast of sounds that give it substance, silence here would be nothing more than black, empty darkness. The wind, that gigantic sound-crushing wheel, gives it all its depth. When it dies down, or is quiet, it brings out the magnificent, hidden monotony of Desolation, as in Piranese's *Prisons* where the silence of the bottomless pits allows sighs, moans, and mysterious bursts of air to rise to the surface. The silence of Kerguelen speaks a dignified language. It has a solemn, heartrending sound that the wind's chatter never quite manages to stifle. This sonority comes from somewhere deep and dark within the ruins. It has transmitted its depth to the dead stones and the fallen columns.

The pact with darkness and the abyss has forever been sealed between the stone and the silence of Kerguelen. When you put your ear to the surface of the rocks, you can make out a noise coming at quick regular intervals, like the rasping sounds the prisoner hears from his small barred window. It's the dull grinding of a pulley. You would think the noise was escaping from every pore of the rock like a rolling millstone. Sound is imprisoned, making the night seem so oppressive that I feel liberated hearing the sea endlessly rolling in.

At the end of the thirties, there wasn't a living soul on Desolation, as if men wanted to avoid the archipelago as war approached. But when it did happen, other men came to seek refuge on the once more uninhabited island.

On 14 December 1940, a small boat sent out from a ship waiting on the open sea came towards the coast. The silence was so disturbing that the detachment thought it was a trap. The nine seamen were soldiers, but dressed in civilian clothes. Weapons were hidden at the bottom of the boat, ready to be used at the slightest warning. When they were close to shore, the leader noticed some barracks and, in the middle of the huts, something moving. As they were slowly picking up their weapons, they saw the shape move again: it was a sea elephant.

These men were from the *Kriegsmarine* and the ship waiting for them out at sea was one of the most famous German raiders, the *Atlantis*, under the command of the Captian Rogge, later Admiral Rogge. The *Atlantis* had just sunk an English cargo boat in the Gulf of Bengal, its thirteenth victim. "Strike, then disappear" was the law of the chase. The raider disguised as a cargo ship had not touched land. Fresh water was beginning to run out and the *Atlantis* needed a certain amount of repair. Where could they drop anchor? It was important to find a place out of reach of British lines of communication. It was then that Rogge remembered the German mission to Kerguelen; he even had the maps made by the *Gazelle* in 1874. The *Atlantis* dropped anchor on the central coast of the island, at the entrance to Foundry Arm. Rogge was worried, as he feared the English might be occupying the island.

The man in charge of the landing party, Ulrich Mohr,

published an account of this stay on the island in the *Berliner illustrierte Zeitung* of 26 March 1942.[9] Looking over the base at Port Couvreux, he describes a similar scene to Rallier du Baty at the observatory camp. He is struck by the haste of the former occupants who left everything just where it was. There was a calendar on the wall with a pretty blonde drinking Pernod. The calendar had stopped at 8 November 1936. Strangely enough, half a round loaf of bread was still intact. Mohr reports that it was still edible.

Having been informed that there was no further danger, the *Atlantis* proceeded into Foundry Arm. The ship struck a rock, putting a hole in the steel hull. The *Atlantis* ran aground and could not move. For three days they tried everything to free the ship. The cargo was moved and they tried to get the *Atlantis* off the rock with the combined force of the engines and the tide, but nothing worked. Rogge himself put on a diving suit and went down to see how serious the situation was and came back aghast: the *Atlantis* was literally impaled on the rock. Would he be forced to stay on Kerguelen for the whole of the war because of a stupid accident? It was then, on the third night, that the wind came to his rescue. The storms were so violent that the ship made a sudden heave. That wasn't the end if its difficulties as the storm was sending the boat towards the shore and the hidden shoals. The *Atlantis* miraculously managed to get out of danger and enter Gazelle Basin, where they carried out repairs over several days.

A tragedy struck on Christmas Eve. A sailor called Bernhard Herrmann was painting the ship's funnel when he fell and died of an embolism four days later. You can still see his grave near the waterfall where the *Atlantis* took their water: 1000 tons of "the purest and freshest water ever drunk," according to Mohr.

The Germans collected some of the famous Kerguelen cabbage. But they made the mistake of cooking it. The cabbage smelled so awful, it seems, that the whole ship stank of it. On 10 January 1941, the *Atlantis* left Gazelle Basin under another name, the *Tamesis*, a harmless commercial vessel built in Danzig just before the war. Steaming north, the false *Tamesis* sank the British cargo boat *Mandasor* off the Seychelles two weeks later. However, on 22 November 1941, it was the *Atlantis'* turn to be sent to the bottom near Ascension Island. A few months later, Kerguelen was to be the hideout of other German raiders, the *Komet* and the *Pinguin*.

In a letter to Gracie Delépine, Ulrich Mohr gives some interesting particulars on the *Atlantis'* clandestine stay on Kerguelen. He had suggested to his superiors that they should use Kerguelen to store precious cargo "instead of uselessly sinking it."

I've always found this last detail disconcerting, especially after discovering a novel by Alan Sillitoe, *The Lost Flying Boat*. The author of *The Loneliness of the Long-distance Runner* writes about the adventure of six ex-RAF pilots who went to Kerguelen in a seaplane looking for a U-boat with a cargo of Nazi gold that had been sunk in a fjord of the archipelago during the war.

"We came through a three dimensional archipelago of cloud and sighted the jagged basalt inlets of northern Kerguelen. [...] He felt as if he had taken part in creating the splashed shape of this island by the fact of his own birth, which he was revisiting after decades of painful absence. Mine, all mine."

Alan Sillitoe has evidently never set foot on Kerguelen. The islands and bays he mentions are nearly all imaginary. And yet the atmosphere of Desolation Island is superbly recreated. Sillitoe has understood the strange complicity of wind and silence. He expresses it through one of his characters, the narrator, whose profession revolves precisely around sound. The hero, who is the wireless operator on the seaplane, flies above Kerguelen, drawn by the song of space. In spite of his headphones, the crackling static, and whistling air, he perceives the extraordinary depth of Kerguelen's peace.

But the most surprising thing of all is Sillitoe's very approach to the subject. He obviously chose Kerguelen because it sounded strange, fantastic. He decided that the fortune in gold could only be found in a place like that, which is strangely similar to Mohr's idea of making it a treasure island. For Sillitoe, the Nazi gold is simply a metaphor for the only Eldorado worth searching for: adventure. But, as the hero says in the end, "God drives a hard bargain. You live a dream, then you have to pay for it."

"Finish your work, make your way home." The Chevalier de Kerguelen appreciated these lines hailing his triumphal return only too well. He knew, however, that his fate had been realized on 12 February 1772, when he saw the dismal "continuation of land." He finally came to believe something he had not seen. Kerguelen *took another dive*—there are no other words for it— like someone who has just got out of an awkward situation and can't stop himself from tripping up again. Nevertheless, he had a narrow escape the first time. He had almost got out of trouble when a terrible doubt assailed him: perhaps I didn't see it properly. These scholars who talk to me about noble savages and enchanted islands are probably right. Then he went back and looked behind him. Like Eurydice, France in the southern ocean dies a second time. "No one having put his hand to the plow, and looking back, is fit for the kingdom of God." (Luke)

There are only two portraits of Yves de Kerguelen in existence. The first shows a young man in a lieutenant's uniform, in a slightly languid pose, as befits a contemporary of King Louis XV. His hand lies flat in his waistcoat, and his wig with its excessively heavy sides makes him seem rather frail. His eyes have a gentle but penetrating look. The face is pleasing, with a hint of shyness. The tightly closed lips and the pointed chin express a certain hidden stubbornness. The most noticeable feature is the nose, which goes to the left. This crooked nose may well spoil the symmetry of the face, but it gives Kerguelen an unusual, winning charm.

The other painting, in the Château de Trémarec, is so different that one has the impression of looking at another man. The nose, which so appealingly went on a spree to one side, now hardly departs at all from the rest of the face. The dark look in the eyes has a rather disturbing gleam, which the fleshier features still don't soften. Although the expression on his face is noble, something violent and domineering can also been seen in it. Those eyes, which are capable of cold anger, nonetheless have a melancholy look, a sadness that one keeps to oneself. This portrait was painted between the two voyages, when Kerguelen was at the height of his glory. There is the dazzled look of someone who has come out into the light too quickly.

There is another portrait hanging in the Château de Tré-marec: it is a painting of his wife, Marie-Laurence de Bonte, who came from a rich, noble Dunkirk family. Kerguelen had married her in 1758. Very little is known about their life together. He had met her when he was sent on a mission to this Flanders Port. No doubt he had chosen her himself, as he was head of the family since his father's death in 1750. What can one make of her delicate air and the fond look in her eyes?

She died in 1784. The opening sentences of her will are surprising. They contain scarcely veiled reproaches regarding her elusive husband: "I beg Mr. de Kerguelen to remember his early upbringing and the virtuous precepts his highly respectable mother gave him. [...] I pray the Almighty to enlighten the precious moments remaining to Mr. de Kerguelen so that he will reflect on his conduct to good purpose."[10]

On the subject of her children, she adds: "My maternal love has cost me many tears thinking of all the hopes for their futures destroyed."

Absorbed as he was by his passion, did Kerguelen drag his family down with him? He is a Faustian character who resolves to accept the final catastrophe and remain silent. What kind of pact did he sign? "You live a dream, then you must pay for it."

6

Departure at dawn for Port-aux-Français. The *Aventure* will stop at Port Raymond then Cemetery Island. Enormously high walls of rock like ramparts with countless waterfalls spilling over them, monumental arenas, large clouds with various light effects unfold like a Gustave Doré landscape all along Saint Malo Cove. Port Raymond is at the end of the bay. The keen morning air has etched every line in the landscape. Halfway along this colossal natural display, the *Aventure*'s engine gets caught in the seaweed, spins and gurgles laboriously, leaving a thick trail of smoke in its wake.

Like most Kerguelen ports, Port Raymond is just an anchorage at the end of a bay with a cabin. It was originally used as a shelter for astronomical observations. It's named after a sailor who died on Kerguelen, Raymond Guillou, whose family name was given to an island in the Morbihan Gulf. He must have been someone well thought of or well liked. We pass a "Quartermaster's Rock." My Delépine book says that this quartermaster was none other than Raymond Guillou.

The boat heads off towards Cemetery Island. The sea looks white with a soft, lazy swell. The surface is like dough gently kneaded by the *Aventure*'s wake. Shoals of seaweed stagnate in the sun. An enormous boat on the water suddenly looms up in the still air. Its very tall hull is showing a lot of space below the Plimsoll line. There is something strange about its position. It's on the water but not floating. It's then I realize that it has run aground on the edge of the shore. It's standing very straight, held on the shingle beach like a ship about to be launched into the sea. A dead ship about to be set afloat is a terrible sight. You would think it was going to come to life again and slide down into the ocean, but this movement you always expect and never see, this suspended resurrection is worse than a death blow. Stained with rust and bird droppings, the ghost ship seems forever held back, suffering a kind of torture of Tantalus, facing the sea that could bring it to life again.

As I approach, I can see the name of the ship, the *Alberta*. This is the very ship that caused Captain Eyssen of the German raider, the *Comet*, one of the greatest scares of his life. Two months after the *Atlantis* has been here, another German ship, also camouflaged as a cargo boat, dropped anchor off Kerguelen on 6 March 1941. Sailing from Bergen in Norway, the *Komet* had achieved the feat of reaching the Pacific and Indian Ocean, not through the Atlantic, but via Siberia and the Bering Strait.

Being cautious, Captain Eyssen also sent a boat ashore; he feared the English might be somewhere in the archipelago. As he approached Cat Island, the commando saw a ship in the distance. He was convinced it was an enemy ship, so his men in the boat hurriedly came back to the *Komet*, which weighed anchor before heading in the direction of the unknown boat. It was then that the Germans realized their mistake: it was only a wreck. "It seemed as though there had been a mutiny on board; or else, had the ship gone aground after the mutiny? We could not find out anything about this ship," Captain Eyssen relates.

We climb inside the *Alberta*. The rudder, the portholes, the ventilators, the bulkheads, everything had been ripped out. Like a Leviathan gutted of its entrails, the ship now looks like nothing more than an empty tank echoing to the clang of our footsteps. The insistent drip, drip, drip of water falling into the flooded hold makes an obsessive kind of music. A colony of cormorants has taken up residence in the prow.

"There was wreckage everywhere, broken knives, objects taken to pieces, navigation equipment deliberately smashed. The crew had obviously gone ashore, but where had they gone? There were rats, " Captain Eyssen reports. He only took a few things from this boat, but later made a positive raid on Port Jeanne d'Arc.

In 1941, the Germans could not understand why there was no one on Kerguelen. The captain of the *Komet* was on his guard for the whole of his stay there. A rendezvous with two other German ships was arranged in the open sea off the coast on 12 March. The *Alstertor* brought twenty-seven postal sacks from Germany for the *Komet*. The other was a raider, the *Pinguin*, which hunted enemy ships in Southern Georgia.

The next day, the *Pinguin* anchored in the Gazelle Basin. The ship's log notes the following reaction on seeing Kerguelen: "The sailors are silent at the sight of all these rocks without land; the atmosphere seems hostile, and this forsaken enemy place, lashed by storms, does not please the men at all."

We have this same uneasy feeling after our visit. The ghost ship with its name on the hull is deceiving us. It's not the *Alberta* we have before us, but the *Esperance*. The second name of the ship has been half-obliterated, but you can still make it out, as in a palimpsest. It's the older one that has remained; the paint must have been more resistant. The

Alberta was a Belgian ship, bought by the Bossière brothers' Austral Fisheries in 1928 to assist the *Austral*. It ran aground in 1931 and was put out of action in 1941 by the cruiser *Australia*. This Australian ship had come to lay mines in channels or anchorages that could be used by enemy ships. We are actually not far from the area where the magnetic mines were laid.

A few minutes later we go ashore on Cemetery Island. Little waves roll the pebbles on the shore, making them clink like glass marbles. I know there is a sailors' cemetery somewhere on the island. After walking for about half an hour I think I can see a field of monoliths. These stones stuck in the ground are really only pieces of wooden planks. With their rounded tops, they are a fairly good imitation of gravestones in English cemeteries. The hillock where these graves stand in a row is nicely sheltered within an inlet and also protected by a small island with cliffs falling sheer into the sea.

While I'm trying to identify these graves, some terns pretend to swoop down on me, shrieking as they dive. I quickly get used to their game. The wind and rain have obliterated the inscriptions apart from a few shapes like spear heads or nails, cuneiform letters impossible to decipher. Out of the fourteen plots, I can only read a few words: "In memory of... Died... " The wooden board has been rasped by the driving rain and whitened by the battering wind. You can see downy grooves in it. These lines give the graves their real meaning; otherwise they are now no more than a worn-down trace of a grave, scarcely a swelling on the surface of the ground. The only inscription that counts is this minutely detailed calligraphy written by the weather. Nature has composed this obituary in her own way on the burial islands. It's the Kerguelen book of the dead.

In a few years, nothing will remain of these mounds adapting themselves to the ground around them until they blend into the pebbly landscape. When he visited the place in 1909, Rallier du Baty had noticed that some crosses were decorated with anchors made out of copper nails, which are no longer there today. He was very much affected by the epitaph of a child of ten, "a poor little cabin boy come so far to die."

Cemetery Island (*île du Cimetière*) used to be called Grave Island. Many English names were simply translated into French. Many German place names left by scientific missions were treated less conscientiously. During the First World War, the names of Bismarck, Roon, Kaiser, and Kronprinz were removed. Baudissin Arm was left because no one knew it was named after a German admiral of Huguenot descent.

PART FOUR

Christmas Harbor

"Knowing a dream is futile will not make it disappear."

Jean Grenier
Les Îles Kerguelen

I

As we travel along the south side of the Courbet Peninsula, I'm thinking, with some apprehension, about my trip to Christmas Harbor. Here I am back at Port aux Français. We're starting from the beginning again. It's as though I were arriving here for the first time on the *Marion*. The base has the same unappealing look that had disappointed me so much a few weeks earlier.

Stepping on to land, I'm greeted by odors I'd forgotten: frying smells from the kitchens wafting on the wind; stale, stuffy smells typical of places without women, like barracks or boys' schools. Catching sight of myself in the mirror, I realize I'm beginning to look like a real Kerguelian. I've got a bushy beard, the frizzy hair of a walker used to being out in the rain, and the garb of a southern ocean Robinson Crusoe who had patched up his clothes with whatever was at hand. It's not that the Kerguelians let themselves go; they don't really observe each other or else they think that no one is looking at them.

I receive an invitation from the voluntary assistants (VATs) in the Technical Service. Port aux Français, a male world, is governed by the ritual of the aperitif. There is an active social life that takes place in about ten different locations. Every building is allocated to a group or profession and each of the men on the winter mission has a room to himself. My building,

L8, is occupied by the crew of the two helicopters; L7 is the Navy building; L4 houses the geophysicists. Apart from the dining hall, which is deserted outside of mealtimes, there is no common room where the men can meet.

The VATs of the Technical Service are mechanics, carpenters, electricians, and garage mechanics. They envy the scientists who are always off on a *manip* field trip while they themselves have to stay on the base to look after the equipment. Everything falls into disrepair: worn-out door frames, broken hinges, windows out of plumb, blocked plumbing.

"Port aux Français is the home of modified makeshift repairs. Every mission has to tinker with the tinkering of the previous mission so that the next one can have its turn at tinkering," says one of my hosts with a laugh.

We are sitting around a heavy wooden table. One of the walls is covered by a huge photo of a forest floor in autumn with soft light filtering through the foliage.

The *plat du jour*: reindeer. The meat is full of flavor although rather stringy. It tastes like venison but less gamey. The dining hall is in a metal hut of one huge, soulless room in spite of a country-style bar at the far end. The men don't linger very long in this refectory after the meal is over. Telegrams announcing the end of the Gulf War are stuck on the wall. No one comments on them. A VAT shrugs his shoulders.

"I came to Kerguelen to get away from television. What a relief not seeing the eight o'clock news! Back home you feel you should look at it." I registered that "back home," which he must have left several months ago.

Before returning to my room, I pay a visit to the base library set up in the former weather station. It's a nice wooden building from the earliest days of Port aux Français. This last relic of the past, which was nearly destroyed a few years ago, is the only thing of any aesthetic appeal in the southern ocean village. It's looked on as the center of the base.

A tracked vehicle stranded there recalls more heroic days. The *Weasel*, designed mainly for snow, didn't suit Kerguelen. The tracks wore out very quickly as they were not meant to travel over stony wastes. A roundabout has been put in around the old weather station and below it a Charles de Gaulle Square with a flagpole and tricolor flag. Needless to say, it's flapping proudly in the wind—so proudly in fact that it's soon torn to shreds. But the base has a plentiful stock of flags.

The library smells of old paper, dust, and that musty iodine smell of seaside villas shut up in winter. The books are not often disturbed on their shelves. Many of the paperbacks go back to the fifties. I'm quite touched to find covers with naïve drawings and authors I didn't expend to see here: Rosamond Lehmann, Elizabeth Goudge, Daphne du Maurier. But more than anything else, it's the wheat-loft smell and the murmuring of the wind through the windows that bring back these lost impressions. Does one have to come to Kerguelen to recover the past? Opening these dried-out books with their obsolete covers is like taking the stopper out of an old perfume bottle. I unseal them and with my fingers, prize apart the pages stuck together from the damp. The heady odor of a box of colored pencils rises up from the paper, the smell of my pencil case and my eraser when I was a schoolboy. It's from the glue that exudes from the worn spines of the old volumes.

I go out, and the squall soon brings me down to earth again. The base is lit by street lamps with round globes that seem to flicker in the strong wind. You think they might go out, but their light never fails. The chapel of Our Lady of the Winds stands a little apart from the base. It's lit by a cold, white light that emphasizes the severity of the plain cube shape in the style of concrete churches built in the beginning of the sixties.

Port aux Français is saved from incurable dreariness by the proximity of the mountains and the sea. The pointed summit of Mount Ross, the highest peak in Kerguelen (6,000 feet), forms an elegant boundary to the low-lying coast on which the base is built. This mountain is a circumflex accent opportunely placed against the waste ground of the remote, southern ocean village. It makes a statement, gives emphasis, and attracts the attention. It's a landmark, a point that used to be a sign in the old days of the navy and helped to guide ships. The sea is an integral part of the village. As there is no steep drop into the sea, the waves roll in and find no resistance as they hit the shore.

Port aux Français is like a sheet with stones placed on it at random to keep it down, and one day it will fly away in the wind.

Voices wake me up during the night. It's three o'clock in the morning. Groups of people are calmly talking to each other from one building to another. There are beams of light sweeping across the sky like the DCA (Anti-Aircraft Defense) searchlights in films about the Battle of Britain. They try to cross as if to imprison an airplane. The waves of light shine stealthily, then reappear a little farther away. I'm filled with wonder at the sight of these flashes of light that trace quick, brief lines in the sky like the filaments of electric bulbs that still remain incandescent for a few seconds after they have been switched off. Our enthusiasm reaches its peak when the outside lights suddenly go out. The electricians at the power plant decided to do this so that we could get a better view of the night sky.

My first aurora australis...

2

Christmas Harbor has become an obsession. All I can think of is the torn-out eye of the Arched Rock described by Edgar Allan Poe. This bay, where Rochegude went ashore on Kerguelen's second voyage, is one of the most remote in the archipelago. It's very difficult to enter. The northwest region is the least known part of the main island, Grande Terre. The helicopter is my last chance. I've been told there might be a rotation in the next few days. But I'll have to get permission from the *disker*.... Could I possibly have learned to be patient? At any rate, I've lost my impatience. By playing a sort of game with myself, I've managed to separate my anticipation from the normal passage of time. One entertainment I've thought up for myself: as with a carousel, if you miss a turn, the opportunity will always come up the next time around. These are the pathetic little tricks one uses to dodge time's nasty bolts from the blue. The refusal to tackle the enemy head-on requires constant attention and mental agility; it's a useless battle that finally uses up your energy.

The engraving by Williams of the *Terror*, which came to

Kerguelen in 1840 with the *Erebus*, for me denotes the eternal return. It reproduces a catastrophe that didn't eventuate. The brigantine, with the sailors hauling as hard as they can on the sails, is shown skimming the Arch and turning to windward on the starboard tack, in great danger of being driven into the cliff. The ship was actually saved at the last minute from being wrecked.

Six years later, the *Terror* and the *Erebus* would disappear in the Antarctic. No trace of them has ever been found.

The Arch interests me more than the three-master. Nearly one thousand feet—twice as high as the *Arc de Triomphe!* The first navigators entering Bird Bay (*la baie de l'Oiseau*) all described their amazement at the sight of this monumental portico. "There are several harbors, of which Christmas Harbor is the most convenient," Edgar Allan Poe assures us. Actually, Christmas Harbor is the worst anchorage in Kerguelen, but for two centuries, ships have not been able to resist dropping anchor there. The huge "carriage entrance," as Pagès, an officer on the second voyage called it, attracts sailors from far and wide.

Its architect was the sea, but its foreman, the wind, was the one who performed most of the task. Accurate work well carried out and which took Sir James Clark Ross' breath away. The man who led the first scientific expedition to Kerguelen was also in command of the *Erebus* and the *Terror*. The two ships stayed sixty-eight days in Christmas Harbor where a hut was built for taking magnetic observations. One of the scientists on the expedition, Dr. McCormick, was the first to establish that in ancient times Kerguelen was covered with forests.

He found whole fossilized tree trunks on the nearby Mount Havergal. As he was a practical joker, he pretended they were the remains of a fire lit by Cook seventy years earlier.

I'm surprised to discover two trees in Port aux Français. They are huddled against the side of a barrack building, protected by the wall as though they were behind armor plating. They are two Lambert cypresses, a salt-resistant species quite common on the coast of Brittany. Their scaly leaves spread out against the wall. These trees look like little animals snuggled against their mother, terrified of poking their noses out. Their tops have been cut off by the wind at exactly the same height as the roof. Not one branch has managed to grow higher.

In 1976 and 1977, someone had the weird idea of introducing into Kerguelen a tropical tree, the filao, and a few species of conifer. This ridiculous endeavor ended as a costly failure.

The next thing I discover is the Port aux Français hothouse. Rows of tomatoes, lettuces, and cucumbers flourish under two plastic domes. The VAT market gardener also shows me parsley, thyme, mint, and sorrel. When the nights are very cold, an alarm turns on the heating. The lettuces grow in a month and a half. But the gardener is most proud of the forty to sixty pounds of tomatoes he picks every day.

"Everyone blames the wind, but the soil is just as bad. It's very acidic and I have to sweeten it with lime. The boat used to bring soil here. That's forbidden now. I have to make do with chicken manure."

Port aux Français is so spread out that vehicles had to be brought in. The drivable track ends two and a half miles from the base. There's nothing beyond the weather station and the geophysical building. The marshy plain of the Courbet Peninsula extends as far as the eye can see, dotted with ponds like those of the Dombes area in Burgundy.

Owning a Renault 4 is a sign of importance here. You don't have to know how to drive well, but you do have to know how to park properly. You can park anywhere as along as you are careful to have the door facing into the wind. A while ago my driver parked at the weather station without paying attention to the direction of the wind. His door was ripped straight off and flew up into the air like a sheet of paper. I heard it fall and bounce on the stones that shine as though they had been lacquered. He calmly went off to retrieve it.

"The wind also plays tricks on us here at the weather station. We have the devil's own job measuring precipitation: the rain gauges don't pick up anything—only wind."

My driver draws my attention to a detail that had escaped me: there is no guttering on the roofs in Port aux Français. They are quite useless: the stormy winds are so strong that the rain falls horizontally. The man speaking to me, who is a meteorologist, tells me about the records: the wind often reaches the famous threshold of 160 miles per hour. Their apparatus can't measure its speed above that. In 1970 it seems to have beaten the absolute record of 180 miles per hour. My companion assures me that there is no more rain here than in Paris (an average of 32 inches) and that Port aux Français has slightly more sun than the town of Lille.

There are some buildings going up near the weather station for use by the CNES (*Centre National d'Etudes Scientifiques*). It will be a solid construction, the most modern on the base, whereas the other buildings are mostly made of molded fibro-cement panels on a metal framework. The foreman, who is in charge of a team of workers from Réunion, comes down from the scaffolding. He curses the wind that is intent on sabotaging his work.

"You'd think it had cast a spell on the concrete. I have to keep wetting it, as the wind dries it out all the time and makes it crack."

You get the best view of the whole of the base from this half-finished building. Now I understand why the site of Port aux Français is so unattractive. In the beginning they wanted to make a landing field out of it. The project never went ahead. But the day will come when planes will touch down at Port aux Français. Then the Kerguelen I'm coming to know will no longer exist. I feel a sudden rush of feeling for the dullness and haphazardness of the little southern ocean village.

I come back on foot along the shore. Suddenly the rocks start to move: they're not rocks but sea elephants waking up and grunting as though they mean business. One of them starts lumbering towards me with his monstrous mouth wide open, then stops in his tracks, winded with the effort. He collapses back into the mud, stretches out, and yawns. He must weigh at least three tons. I move forward rather gingerly into their wallow. There are dozens of them lying there grumbling in their sleep or snoring loudly. For the moment they are harmless, but they can be dangerous in the mating season.

Every male has his own harem, but as there are ten times fewer females, the pasha has to fight to keep them. In October, the male spends his time warding off rivals that try to impregnate the females as soon as he has his back turned. Sea elephants fight with frenzy. Their scarred hides bear huge bite marks.

I have an appointment with the *disker* at the Residence. This building stands a little way from the base, on the higher ground. The Kerguelen family coat of arms, "Ever green," adorns the front of the house. Near the entrance stand two huge cauldrons used by the whalers in the old days to render the fat. The interior is furnished in the style of a fighting soldier who has come into money, with its ship's chest, deep armchairs, curios, and engravings on the wall.

The *Pléiade* edition of Balzac's *Comédie Humaine* is displayed on a set of shelves.

I've got permission! The *disker* has told me that he will do his best to get me to Christmas Harbor by helicopter. "It will depend on the weather." He doesn't seem too put out by having a rival to his authority, showing the indulgent fatalism of the old colonial civil servant, experienced in dealing with men and the climate.

The *disker* is chosen by the TAAF (French Southern and Antarctic Territories) administration after a series of interviews and tests. There are a lot of candidates. The area managers are usually soldiers, but it's not obligatory. Managing a mission comprising scientists as well as soldiers and VATs is not an easy job. Port aux Français is not an army barracks. Although the people on the winter mission have agreed to a year's exile, they're not inclined to put up with the oppression of a hierarchy.

As I'm about to take my leave of the governor of Kerguelen, I notice a long stack of files tied with a strap in another room. The *disker* saw where I was looking.

"They're the Kerguelen archives. Each file contains the mission report that every *disker* has to compile before he leaves. No one reads them."

Night has fallen over Port aux Français with the noises that are now quite familiar: the whining of the power station, the piercing cries of the seagulls. And the wind, that gigantic machine that gives us silence.

A man with a shaven head comes and stands in front of me under the light of a street lamp. The razor has left a slight trace of some bluish patches on the top of his skull.

"Don't you recognize me?"

He puts on his cap: it's "the poor sailor."

"Are you still unhappy?"

"Me? Unhappy?"

I remind him of our conversations on board the *Marion*. He looks at me coldly. No, I don't recognize "the poor sailor." He doesn't seem himself. His voice shows no emotion. Its tone has changed as though his voice was breaking.

Back in my room, I've turned the radio on to FM. The Kerguelen station plays rock music. Idle hours... The announcer has a deep voice. He mumbles some strange words. I can't understand a thing. I picture him in his studio announcing each new record to the seventy listeners in Port aux Français, trying to sound confidential, trying out some words that are popular again like *disc jockey*. He's probably a VAT.

In any event, what he's saying becomes more and more disjointed. I can only make out an indistinct flow of words. Then the voice dies.... All that's left are whistling noises and a hissing over the frequency every few seconds. What's happening? I come out of my room, curious to find out.

"Did you hear the radio?" I said to my neighbor.

"The radio!" he replied, rolling his eyes.

"Where do they broadcast from?"

"From the geophysical building. What's the matter?"

I explain why I'm worried. He goes to get a car. The geophysical building, where I was earlier this afternoon, is outside the perimeter of the base.

We arrive at the geophysical laboratory a few minutes later. A man with a beard, wearing the traditional greenish yellow Kerguelen parka greets us and bursts out laughing when I ask him where the studio is.

"There's no studio. Come with me."

He takes us into a room where a broken tape on a console is twisting around, hitting against the spool.

"There's no announcer. They're old tapes recorded heaven knows when. We keep broadcasting them indefinitely. Some tapes are so worn that they finally break, like this evening. It's not the music or the voice that interests people; it's just for background noise."

So the voice with the terrible diction was just from an old tape recording. I have to laugh at my mistake. But is it really so funny: a radio humming away endlessly like a top to the complete indifference of everyone on the base?

3

The helicopter should be leaving for Christmas Harbor in six days. I'll only be able to stay there for an hour as my transport has to leave again almost immediately for Port aux Français. One hour is not very long, but for someone who has looked forward to it so much, it will be as long as all that waiting. It will be the high point of my stay, which is due to end the following day.

I spend my days in the library while I wait for the helicopter. I make a few interesting discoveries there including a strange book by Valéry Larbaud called *The Governor of Kerguelen*, published by the Nouvelle Revue Française in 1933. It's actually about Christmas Harbor (the author of *Barnabooth* calls it *Port-Noël*). The idea for the book comes from the well-known literary game: "If you had to spend the rest of your life on a desert island, which twenty books would you take with you?" Valéry Larbaud imagines a French civil servant, once in a very senior position and now out of favor: "You have had the misfortune to offend those in high places, but taking into account the fact that you are a man of considerable ability, you will simply be banished for a while and appointed for one... three... five years (that's the maximum) as governor of Kerguelen, residing at Christmas Harbor, the principal town of that colony."

This senior civil servant is also notified that he should take only a few books, of which some must be chosen from the ten Spanish comedies of the Golden Century; Boileau's two satires, etc. To add to the governor's misfortune, it is decided that "commentaries, glossaries, and other reference works are only permitted if he can prove they are indispensable." Valéry Larbaud even wonders whether these constraints might not be too generous to the governor, so he has the idea of making him take "the ten most boring books he has read."

What excites my curiosity in this short text is the way Larbaud imagines Kerguelen and above all his idea of linking it with "perpetual exile" and a "dearth of books." He was also fascinated by the place and located his governor in Christmas Harbor. Larbaud doesn't mention the Arch but seems well informed about Kerguelen. He sees it as a "desert island," which was actually true when he was writing the work. In 1933 Kerguelen had already been abandoned for two years. He had probably heard about the Bossière affair, which was in the papers at that time.

Larbaud, who has played "the governor's game" himself, lists *The Divine Comedy* among the books he would take with him. The further I go, the more the various trails converge, as if a mysterious hand were drawing facts and coincidences in the same direction so that they arrive at the same end.

I can imagine the scene: the governor with his hands behind his back, gazing at the Arch on a dull winter afternoon. "The French pay enough taxes to decently house the governor, install central heating in his residence in Christmas Harbor and draught-excluders on the double and quadruple windows. He will have a fine uniform lined throughout with little electric warmers, a well-stocked cellar, an ultramodern bathroom, a hothouse [...] and he can eat the usual fare with provisions from Madagascar."

With my nose in my book, I pay no attention when the door bangs. A man comes in. I've already seen him somewhere. It's the scientist I met on my first trip on the *Aventure*, the man who told me about the sheep on Long Island. He's amused by my obsession.

"There's nothing to see at Christmas Harbor. You're wasting your time."

He seems more talkative this time and admits to me that he came to Kerguelen for the first time in 1961 to finish his military service here. This is his fourth stay and he hadn't been back for fifteen years.

I asked him some questions about his early days in the archipelago.

"A detachment of airforce engineers had built Fillod barracks. It was rudimentary but not as dismal as the present base. There was no *disker*, only the chief officer of the mission." He adds, wryly, "We felt we really were entrusted with a mission then." He's not very forthcoming about his life on Kerguelen. I sense there are things he doesn't want to reveal. There seems to be an episode during his stay in the archipelago that he doesn't want to talk about.

We walk along together in the direction of the "postal center." The cindery, shiny ground looks as though it has been tarred. What use can a post office possibly be in a country where postal deliveries take place only a few days a year? To buy stamps of the French Southern and Antarctic Territories? This series is highly sought after by philatelists, who all know the Kerguelen Islands and dream of one day owning a "Résidence de France," an extremely rare cover from the Bossière period. Every member of the mission has the right to send a weekly telegram of seventy words to a correspondent of his choice.

The postal center is the only place in the archipelago where you take out your wallet. Kerguelen, the cashless society. You can buy everything at the cooperative (alcohol, cigarettes, clothes, shoes), without having to pay with cash or even by check. Anything bought is taken off the salary at the end of the tour of duty. I did notice, though, that the merest trifle has a price, often inflated, and is the object of quite keen bargaining: chalcedony, opals, lacquered fish heads, reindeer antlers, etc.

"You've made the acquaintance of our hero, have you?" says the meteorologist who lost the car door.

"What hero?"

"The man you were talking to a moment ago, Georges Polian. He climbed Mount Ross in 1975. He's a notable figure in Kerguelen, one of those who knows the archipelago best. He made reconnaissance trips to places where no one else had ever been. He could tell you a lot."

A genuine Kerguelian! The species is too rare to be allowed to escape. He has kept a seat for me next to him in the refectory and beckons me over.

"What are these secrets all about? I know you. I've read your accounts of the exploration you've done in the TAAF Review."

"It's ancient history.... I was young and thoughtless. Rather than me telling you the story of my life, why don't you come to Port Couvreux with me for a *manip*? We'll come back via the Courbet Peninsula to see the penguin rookeries."

"It's impossible. I don't want to miss Christmas Harbor."

"You'll be back in time. As I told you before, Christmas Harbor isn't at all interesting"

I hesitate. I don't particularly want to go to Port Couvreux, but what would I do for six days at Port aux Français?

"All right, I'll come. Is it true that you were the first man to explore certain parts of the archipelago?"

"Yes. I've even named a few lakes and valleys."

"How many?"

"I haven't counted them.... Perhaps a hundred."

"How did you choose the names?"

He gives a vague wave of the hand.

"I can't remember.... At random."

I suspect that he won't pursue the topic any further and that it would be not only useless but also tactless to insist.

"Do you realize that tomorrow is Easter?" he says, changing the subject. "One forgets everything here."

Easter... Kerguelen perpetuates the Easter service, the struggle between light and darkness. The black, threatening sky becomes light again; the silent words of all those who have died, sleepers who live again in an island or an inlet celebrate resurrection.

Coming out of the dining hall, I meet the *disker* again.

"I'm going to Port Couvreux. May I come and have a look at the archives this evening?"

He's silent for a just a moment, then says, "Come if you like. You can try my cognac."

The old papers in the Residence are almost as delectable as the *disker*'s brandy. Each strap untied is a new year. The old years are the juiciest. I love the feel of the dry transparent paper from the early years, crinkled by heavy-handed typing. All these reports on exercise books or flimsy paper or carbon copies smell of paraffin. You can guess that, for the most part, the practical men who wrote them found it a chore, or even a pain. Nonetheless, they all applied themselves to the task of describing their mission.

Only one seems to have taken any pleasure in it, passing on this piece of advice to his successor: "Keep a log: it is tiresome but irreplaceable. It is like Dangeau's memoirs: there is nothing more boring to read, but when you are looking for a detail of such and such a day at the court of Louis XIV, that is the only place you will find it." (1959-1960 Mission Report)

I discover how the site of Port aux Français was chosen on 19 December 1950 following the decision of the then minister for French Overseas Territories, François Mitterand. The chief officer of the mission describes how these men explored along the Castle River looking for the best land. "We have made our choice.... We will set up here." He justifies his choice in these words: "It is a plateau sufficiently under cover (sic) to protect us from the northwest wind and sufficiently flat to keep excavation work to a minimum."

The 1950 temporary base comprised four prefabricated wooden huts and three living quarters built on site. The chief officer for the 1951 mission passes judgement on the settlement: "It has a heroic character but lacks organization." His successor has a completely opposite point of view: "There is nothing heroic now about a stay in Kerguelen." On the subject of "the mission spirit," he notes that "it is mainly those who don't have it who talk about it most." In his opinion, "central heating and hot running water do not help strengthen the pioneering spirit." Furthermore, he divides those on the winter mission into two categories: "the bourgeois" and "the pioneers."

I thought that no woman had ever spent the winter in Port aux Français. However, in 1955 a certain Captain Peretti had brought his wife to Kerguelen. "Mme. Peretti became the mother of fifty-two boys and the amount of underwear and socks she thought up, made, knitted, and mended is really incredible. Her gentleness and her smile made a significant contribution towards 1955 being a trouble-free year."

As I go through these notes, I realize that the members of these transitory communities have not always lived in harmony. In the confined living conditions of Port aux Français, every event, every incident is blown out of proportion. The disappointment comes through, especially in the reports of the doctors, who try to give a psychological assessment of the departing mission. "An ordinary year with ordinary people." The same doctor, quoting Saint Paul, adds: "Where the Spirit does not dwell, there is death." That was for the year 1959–60.

"We are now being assigned men as though they were going to serve at Carcassonne or Périgeux. That's the price you have to pay for presenting Kerguelen as another Côte d'Azur." This comment comes from the chief officer for the mission of the same year.

There also seems to have been rivalry between soldiers in the technical and the scientific services, who "are keen on retaining one of the signs and prerogatives of the French intellectual: squalor." The *disker* of the thirty-third mission (they were usually numbered after the sixties) writes: "Science is rather like a State within the State. Having their own budget confers a certain autonomy." As for the members of technical services, the *disker* of the twenty-fourth mission has this to say about them: "The purpose of the base they build and inhabit often escapes quite a few of these worthy men who sees no further than their own problems with concrete, leaks, cut cables, farming, and plant propagation." The *disker* of the twenty-seventh confirms that: "It is the running of the place that takes precedence and especially the building; Paris seems to be interested in nothing but the TP (practical work) program."

Why do they come to Kerguelen? Each person has his own explanation. One talks of "a mystique" while another mentions "a Tartarinesque mirage."[1] If there is a legend of Kerguelen, writes the medical man in charge for the year 1960–61, it's "an accommodating legend justifying all organizational anomalies, all inadequate outcomes, and shielding from all criticism. It has the advantage of transforming the simple fact of having lived here into a heroic exploit. [. . .] It's a futile legend because it complicates simple things to no good purpose." The disker of the twenty-fifth mission writes ironically about a "folklore which seeks to glorify the austral animal, a Darwinian notion that the winter mission transforms a man and that evolution is always to his advantage if not to his glory." The *disker* of the thirtieth mission claims: "The general comfort of all has killed the community spirit. PAF (Port aux Français) is no longer a mission: it is an establishment housing civil servants who work and think like civil servants." The *disker* of the thirty-third mission deplores the fact that his predecessor left him 6,000 liters of wine.

This Courtelinesque aspect of Kerguelen life is often in evidence.[2] One of the *diskers* makes the observation the "Port aux Français is not the base for a scientific or meteorological mission, but the district administrative capital more directed towards the exegesis of administrative documents than towards scientific observation." The disker of the twenty-seventh mission states with some bitterness: "Everyone criticizes the same deficiencies, raises the same problems, puts forward the same solutions, and all make it plain in advance that they are convinced they will not be heeded."

The doctor on the thirty-third mission makes the same criticism: "If a project does exist, everything proceeds as though it had been taken over by some far-off authority in Paris that defines down to the last detail the activities and living conditions on the base: the use of vehicles, the consumption of butter, etc."

These reports that keep describing the same disenchantment through the years have nothing more to tell me. As one of them says: "You arrive in Kerguelen full of good resolutions, determined to do better than your predecessors; you leave somewhat disillusioned, but happy in the end if you have succeeded in doing as well." None of them says anything about the islands, apart from the *disker* of the thirty-fifth mission, who concludes his report with these words: "I have experienced the best and the worst. The best is the wild, grandiose beauty of these islands. The worst, the pettiness of the men, so out of place in this setting."

The present *disker* is putting his papers in order in the other room. What will he write when his turn comes at the end of his mission in eight months? I suddenly hear his chair scraping on the floorboards. He gets up and comes towards me.

"Did you find what you were looking for?"

"Yes. I've read almost everything."

"Did you learn anything?"

"A lot. I've realized there's no such thing as a happy *disker.*"

"Happy! We aren't sent here to be happy."

"One of your predecessors wrote this: 'The disker is condemned to solitude.'"

"What was I this evening if not a man alone? This evening, like all the other evenings. That's my lot. I'm not complaining."

No sooner has the door of the Residence closed behind me, than I'm whipped by the wind. Port aux Français is struggling against it. When I was inside behind the double windows, I had no idea of the wildness of the wind. The gravel rises up like a wave. The wind, in a fury, has unleashed its hounds. I can feel it hunting around in the metal framework to find the weak point. I sense it ready to leap at its prey's throat and tear it to pieces. While reveille sounds in my ears, the abandoned base is being shaken almost senseless in its jaws and seems to beg for mercy.

4

"And entering the tomb, they saw, a young man clothed in a long white robe sitting on the right side; and they were alarmed. But he said to them: 'Do not be alarmed. You seek Jesus of Nazareth, who was crucified. He is risen!'"

There are about twenty of us present in the Chapel of the Winds for the Easter service improvised by some of the people on the winter mission. All the men on the base from Réunion are present. After listening to the passage from St. Mark and St. John, we find we are quickly running out of readings. The absence of a priest makes this religious service seem a little awkward, but what we lack in skill we make up for in fervor.

There is something naïve about the chapel, just like our liturgical impromptu. The floor is uneven, as the side aisles are paved with big round black stones collected in the archipelago. Artificial flowers grace the fourteen stations of the cross. The dark transept is covered with plaques giving thanks for answered prayers. Only the severe face of an ancient wooden sculpture of Christ saves the whole place from a certain religious sentimentality.

Several marble plaques have been put up on the walls: "16 December 57—Marriage of Marc Pechenart and Martine Raulin; on the same day, Martine Pechenart laid the first stone of Our Lady of the Winds." This wedding is the only one that has ever taken place in Kerguelen. The couple now live in Concarneau.

Another plaque, a little farther along: "Jean-Marie Stoll, engineer, geophysicist, died in an accident at Port aux Français on 23 December 1963."

The third states that "Denys Sens, radar technician, twentieth mission, died on 16 March 1970 ."

Like the churches in France, this humble southern ocean chapel smells of wax and that stale odor of dark places and old clothes. Something is missing here: the heavy, acrid smell of incense.

We come out into a real Easter morning; a "winnower's wind," which seems to shake the sun and clean the air, making it clear and transparent. The approach to the chapel is unusual: slabs and tombstones just stuck in the ground. It looks like a Druid mound. This packing together of the graves looks like the funerary hodgepodge around the church at Landudal. The same layout, the same neglect.

All the tombstones in the Landudal church bear the name Kerguelen. The Château de Trémarec close by is in a hamlet of the commune. The discoverer of Desolation Island was not buried at Landudal. He died in Paris in 1797 and is buried in the Père Lachaise cemetery, but I haven't managed to find his grave.

There were seven people at his funeral. Five were deputies of the Council of the Five Hundred. Kerguelen took "the secret of one of the most uneasy souls who ever lived" to the grave with him.[3] As he felt he has been a victim of an arbitrary royal decision, the former Saumur prisoner had greeted the events of 1789 with enthusiasm. "The day the Revolution began was the greatest day of my life," he wrote later in an address to his "fellow citizens." Restored to his position in the Navy in 1793 and promoted to rear admiral the same year, he was appointed as squadron commander at the time of the Quiberon expedition, but discharged soon afterwards. He was imprisoned under suspicion in Brest in 1794, freed after the death of Robespierre, and once again reinstated in the Navy. He was retired after his participation in the questionable engagements at Groix.

Everything was over for Kerguelen when, at the beginning of 1797, there was talk of his being offered the Navy portfolio. These rumors no doubt had the effect of easing the last months of his life. "I feel I am obliged to try and make people forget my disgrace, to make up for my mistakes; I have made them and am so aware of them that I shall remember them to my grave," he wrote in 1775.

His end is like Christopher Columbus'. What could "the dawn visitor" and the pariah who left desolation behind him have in common? They had the same obsessions. Haunted by Eldorado, blinded by what they had read, the two men saw absolutely nothing of what they discovered. "In dire straits, Columbus maintains his will to succeed to the very end, in spite of one disaster after another."[4] Kerguelen showed the same refusal to admit defeat. The only difference is that today Columbus' dream has run its course; Kerguelen's is only just beginning. His discovery is still new, even after two centuries. No dream could be more real than the unknown lakes washing away at the foot of glaciers.[5] This is creation in action, an invitation to travel, not only through space, but also through time.

I'm thinking about Rallier's stoicism, the silence he maintained once he had returned to France. He was a seaplane pilot in the

World War I, during which his brother Henri was killed, as well as Agnès and Bontemps. After that he devoted himself to oceanographic research, travelling to the Azores, Mauritania, and Newfoundland. He never spoke of Kerguelen again. When he was close to retirement, he decided to write his memoirs. Overcome either "by too much modesty or by weariness," he never finished his project.[6] He thought constantly of his sailors and one day wrote this message to them: "I have done the only thing in my power to commemorate your unrecognized hard work: I have given your names to the promontories you weathered against wind and tide."

There is only one proper grave outside the Chapel of the Winds. An Islamic crescent is engraved on the stone. The red mark is disconnected in the middle and has the shape of a lunar E spreading out among the spattered patches of damp, as though the star were bursting through a dull, cloudy sky. This unfinished circle, instead of closing, opens out on to limitless space; could this represent the fate of the man who rests under the only official grave in Kerguelen? His name was Moilimou Bedja. He died at the age of twenty-seven. Who was he? No one knows.

The perimeter of the chapel, built according to the golden section, does not really belong to Port aux Français. This silent retreat dominates the base and the bay from all sides like a foreign blockhouse, looking almost hostile to the world around it. "Ventus est mea vita," the chapel wall proclaims.

Back at the *disker*'s residence, I ask him if he has any information about this Muslim buried behind the chapel.

"They say you're doing a survey of all the graves in Kerguelen."

"All the graves? That would be impossible. I'm only beginning a list of them. I hope my successors will carry on the work."

He goes to a drawer in his desk and takes out a file, which he hands to me after looking at it briefly.

"The Muslim you mentioned was from the Comoro Islands."

The file contains several reports concerning all those who died in Kerguelen since 1950. From one of them, I learn the sad story of Moilimou Bedja, who worked in the kitchens. One day he disappeared. A search was made around the base and his body was finally found, far from Port aux Français. The enquiry shows that he had deliberately gone out to die of hunger and cold. It seems he had a persecution complex. He did not, however, just sink into oblivion. Moilimou Bedja dominates Kerguelen because no one in the Comoros claimed his body. In 1966, the Place Name Commission decided to name an islet in the Baudisson Arm (*Bras de Baudisson*) after him. He stands out alone on the Port aux Français hill, placed according to custom near a place of worship, which, although it was not his own, bears witness to the fact that he is henceforth a person of note.

Jean-Marie Stoll, who was crushed to death by a drum of diesel oil during an unloading operation, also has a small island named after him.

Nothing affects me as much as these inventories of a dead man's possessions that the administration draws up after the event. Between a Swiss army knife and a toothbrush, there are copies of Saint Augustine's *Confessions* and Günter Grass' *Tin Drum.*

What was this clay specialist from Alsace looking for in Kerguelen?

5

Port Couvreux. A fast-moving stream flows by a house. An atmosphere of misfortune and treachery hovers over this little house and garden: it's too neat and tidy. I don't like this thick, almost sticky grass: it's strange and out of place in Kerguelen. There's something poisonous about its lushness. There's something frightening about the ordinariness and dead silence of the abandoned building.

"This is an unlucky place," Georges Polian says, as we are looking at the cross on the top of the hill. For once it doesn't indicate a grave, but danger, a threat. Instead of exorcising Port Couvreux of its demons, it emphasizes the spell.

Port Couvreux has brought bad luck ever since its beginnings in 1912. Shepherds and flocks alike will never take to this bay, which is too isolated and difficult to reach. The sheep left there to run wild during the First World War have never been found. A second attempt was made by the Bossière brothers in 1920. Of the four shepherds who stayed at Port Couvreux between 1922 and 1927, two died.

Three policemen from Le Havre decide to try their luck in Kerguelen in 1927, bringing their families with them. The party consisted of Georges Le Galloudec, his wife, and their little girl Georgette; Pierre Petit and his wife; Léon Ménager, his wife, and their daughter Léone. After a long voyage via the Durban, their ship, the *Lozère*, drops anchor in Port Couvreux. It does not look very appealing. The main shed occupied by the shepherds is filthy. A bad omen: the station flag is at half-mast as one of the colony has just died.[7] With the help of the ship's carpenter, the three men build their house. A few weeks later, they complete the sheep-fold, the laundry, and the bread oven.

They are just beginning to get organized when the three men decide to go seal hunting on Crow Island (*île au Corbeau*) on 29 November. They get lost, their boat breaks down, and they have to spend the night huddled against a cliff. The next day it snows. After the second night in the open, the three men think they have found the way to Port Couvreux, but they don't realize that they are going around in circles.

They clamber through rock falls, wander across a maze of crevasses, hills, and icy streams until they are almost exhausted. Freezing cold and hungry they keep going in the wind and snow. They are following each other at a distance of about one hundred yards, when they suddenly lose sight of each other. Managing to get his bearings, Pierre Petit finally finds the way to the station. He is the first to arrive at Port Couvreux on 3 December, followed a few hours later by Léon Ménager.

Where was Le Galloudec? Each of the men thought he was with the other. The body of the former bicycle policeman from Le Havre was found seventeen days later. He was lying on his back with his arms crossed, his eyes pecked out by the skuas. His grave is away from the house, in the valley, an anonymous cross in the middle of a roughly drawn square, which serves as a cemetery. Port Couvreux, that funereal garden, has room for no other macabre sight but its own; the weed-covered mound of the grave is set well apart.

On 12 February 1928, the *Lozère*, which had called in at Port Couvreux, comes in contact with a raised part of the sea bed in the Gazelle Strait. The crew manages to leave the ship with no casualties and takes refuge in Port Couvreux. These men have nothing to do, and their presence on the station where three women are living causes several incidents. Renée Ménager goes off with one of the sailors from the *Lozère* and disappears somewhere in South Africa.

Aubert de la Rüe and his wife make the acquaintance of the colonists at Port Couvreux in November. The geologist notes that their small flock comprises no more than about thirty head, as several sheep had died during the previous winter. In their well-enclosed and well-sheltered garden, the Robinson Crusoes of Port Couvreux had actually succeeded in growing radishes. "There were among them, surprisingly enough, a few reasonable specimens," Aubert de la Rüe concedes, although he finds these radishes "spindly."

On 23 February 1929, Ménager leaves for France with his daughter Léone, leaving Pierre Petit and his wife behind. You might think that was the end of the adventure for him. Nevertheless, he decides to return to Kerguelen in the same year. "There are things you have to put up with, that's true, but it's a good, free life there." He stays another two years at Port Couvreux.

After the scandal of the men left on Saint Paul in 1931, the last colonists in the history of Kerguelen are hastily put on board the *Austral*. The sheep are abandoned; the three pigs in the barn killed and left there. The German sailors from the *Atlantis*, who paid a visit to Port Couvreux in 1940 discovered the pigs' bodies. To their great surprise, the animals had not rotted, but were "mummified."

The former colonists' verandah has collapsed, but the building is still standing. There are dead birds lying on the wooden floor. The rooms are tiny, like a dolls' house. Also on the ground are a few torn mattresses and a cast-iron stove. The only unusual thing in these cramped quarters is a white-veined black marble fireplace. When I touch it, I realize it's made of wood. One can't help admiring this determination to recreate a middle-class interior in a place as disheartening as this. Nothing predisposed these men and women to leave their country; they came and lived here because they believed in the mirage of Kerguelen. They didn't give up, even though they were deceived. There's a plaster block on the table with this simple inscription: "Pierre Petit, 1927–1930."

Pierre Petit, the original colonist who died in 1970, states that one day when he was with Ménager, he found an iron box in a cave. He opened it with a chisel. The box contained beef with carrots and bully beef left by the Norwegians in 1883. Beside these supplies they found a bottle containing a parchment dated 1772 and signed by Yves de Kerguelen. It was the document claiming the land for France from the first voyage. Instead of taking the document with them, they put it back in the bottle, which they left where they had found it.

Georges Polian finds his way without maps. He takes me to the end of Whalers' Gulf (*le golfe des Baleiniers*), where you can still see the place where supplies were left by the *Eure*. The ship came to Kerguelen in 1893 to confirm French sovereignty over the land. A few stones are all that is left now of a pyramid that, it seems, was ten feet high. At the end of the bay near the channel leading to Fair Weather Harbor (*le havre du Beau Temps*), the remains of a flagstaff are still visible. Three copies of the possession document had been buried at its foot. What has happened to the letters brought by the *Eure*? They were enclosed in weather-proof wrapping, which was then put in a copper box with a securely soldered lid.

In a letter to Gracie Delépine written in 1965, Ulrich Mohr, the chief officer of the *Atlantis*, talks about that stone pyramid. Fifty-year-old food supplies were found buried beneath it and pronounced "perfectly edible." He indicates that the document claiming possession of the islands was hidden under the same pyramid. Mohr asserts that: "We replaced the tins of food taken from the *Atlantis*' stock and put back the stones, not wanting to destroy this means of assistance to any future shipwreck survivors." He makes no mention of the document. It's likely that the Germans took the letter.

The *Eure* left the same documents at Christmas Harbor. On this occasion, the French flag had been raised to the sound of a twenty-one-gun salute. One day, in the hollow of a rock at the top of the Red Dome, Edgar Aubert de la Rüe found a paper dated 17 February 1930, indicating that, unbeknown to all, the Australians had come to explore the southern coast of Kerguelen. They had even used a small seaplane they had brought with them. It was the BANZ (British, Australian & New Zealand) Antarctic Research Expedition led by Sir Douglas Mawson.

We find a cross near the ruins of the pyramid. It's the grave of the soldier Herrmann, who died on 29 December 1940, according to the inscription on a copper plaque. Of all the graves I've seen until now, this is the best kept and the smartest. The German government allocates a sum of money annually to the French authorities for its upkeep. The cross has just been repainted. The grave itself is marked out with a border of white stones. It was located again using directions from Admiral Rogge, who indicated its exact position from a sketch. The cross was in good condition but the weather had obliterated the inscription.

As we make our way towards Port Elisabeth, I question Georges about his ascent of Mount Ross. He tells me that the conquest of this peak was above all a battle against the *diskers* of that time. "When I arrived in 1960, the Ross became an obsession. In Kerguelen, it came to me like a revelation that one of the last virgin lands on the planet was here stretched out before me."

I can picture the enthusiasm of a youth who, a few months earlier, found himself in a disciplinary company deployed along the Tunisian border.

"For a mountain climber like me, used to the alpine world, it was an overwhelming feeling." When I decided to climb Mount Ross, I wanted to find out if there had been any reconnaissance missions in the region. I realized that the interior of Kerguelen was a huge blank. Nothing on the map! Rallier du

Baty, Aubert de la Rüe and the Mouzon mission in 1953 were the only ones who had indicated any landmarks.

"I had found a friend, Georges Rens who, like me, felt impelled to do this. He was the silent type, an ideal climbing companion. When it became clear that the *disker* was not going to give his consent, we mounted a clandestine operation. The big problem was food. We counted on five days walking, so there had to be enough provisions for ten days. There was no way we could carry these supplies as well as the gear. Every time volunteers were requested, we stepped forward so that we could plant a cache of provisions. We stole the food: one of us kept the quartermaster occupied while the other pinched the tins.

We volunteered to go and dig drainage trenches at the Point Molloy underground seismology station. We wielded the pick a few times then left. We managed to reach the Ross crater, but couldn't go any further. That's when we were caught in a very heavy snow storm and held up at Saint Théodule Peak (*le puy Saint-Théodule*). We built low walls and made places to sleep. We even got back to Port aux Français in time. The district commissioner was not fooled and knew we had done the exploration he had forbidden, but he was so relieved to see us again that he said nothing.

"We went on another escapade in September, then again in November: four of us with a worker-priest, Jean Volot. We were going into unknown territory. On the southeastern slope of the Cook Ice-Cap, we discovered a place that had never been explored before. We called it the Diosaz Glacier after a river in Haute-Savoie. One night we bivouacked in a cave with an overhanging entrance. We called it Climbing-Stirrup

Cave (*caverne de l'Étrier*) because we needed a climbing stir-rup with rope, pitons, and snap-hooks to reach it. After camp-ing on the Cook Ice-Cap, we slept for seventeen hours in Climbing Iron Cave. I remember on our way back Jean Volot stopped, amazed, at the sight of a horrible black plain, exclaiming, "It's like something out of Dante." We called it Dante Plain.

"Why take names of places that already exist, like the Diosaz?"

"We always looked for analogies. It was a game we always played."

"On my way to Travers Valley, I crossed Aosta Valley, Grisanche Valley, Courmayeur Valley. Was it you who gave them those names?"

"Yes, I'm the one. We went on that exploration trip in June and September 1961."

"Are there any names that refer to personal memories?"

He hesitates for a moment.

"Yes… You mean intimate memories…. But I didn't want to use Kerguelen to inscribe my personal cartography, as many people did at that time. To me it seemed as stupid as engraving hearts on a tree. I did make one exception, though. A few names, like Alster Valley and Lake Koeslin refer to a German girl from the Hamburg area. She came from eastern Pomerania, from Koeslin, which disappeared from the map after 1945 when it became part of Poland. It was important for me to resurrect that name. The only place it exists now is in Kerguelen."

"And Mount Ross?"

"That was years later.... We finally made it in 1975 thanks to Jean Rivolier, chief medical officer of the Southern Ocean Territories, who organized the expedition."

I scan the man's face. He has possessed the magic power of conferring names. Is it this knowledge of being all-powerful, the awesome impression of having come close to the mystery of creation that made him so reticent at the beginning? He has the thoughtful expression, the off-hand but shrewd authority of the shaman who climbs mountains with ease. He passes lightly and dreamily over the surface of the earth.

No man has ever shed the blood of another in this land we are walking on. Kerguelen, the desolate Eden, has been spared the mark of Cain. Will the words of humans who trap and tame eventually kill the archipelago?

Port Elisabeth. There's no port. Where is Elisabeth? Remains of a Soviet boat washed up on the shore. The cliffs a stone fortress over the abyss. Clouds of seagulls and skuas. Bare, absolutely deserted.

Cape Ratmanoff. Thousands of emperor penguins massed on the beach. The gentleness of the light, like October in France, is a striking contrast to the violence of the waves. The sand like buckwheat flour. I thought I saw a host of people in the distance enjoying themselves in the water. These large shapes stand tall, waddle forward with an air of great importance then dive into the heavy seas with the swaggering, conceited look of the expert swimmer. They are not afraid when I approach them, but I have to crouch down to their height.

Then they form a group, come forward, and form a circle around me. They are so solemn! Their gravity and deference towards me are in sharp contrast with the aversion they show towards each other. They are packed closely against each other, but niggle and quarrel. The moment one steps over into another's territory, they fight and peck. Then slowly, and with great dignity, they come back to their places.

Dismal Point (*Pointe Morne*). A circular landscape of pools and ponds with solid rims. The color of the water displays every shade of yellow: saffron, beige, copper, sienna. The wind had hardened the edges. A rocky outcrop rises up 1,650 feet from the shore: Matley Islet. A limestone rock bearing the name Matley was dug up there in 1963. Parts of a skeleton were found around the grave, blown there by the wind. Rabbits digging their burrows had opened up the grave of this whaling captain who came to Kerguelen at the beginning of the nineteenth century.

The gravestone with this inscription had been sent to Kerguelen by Captain Matley's wife: "To the memory of John Matley, who departed this life on 12 December 1810 when he was in command of the London vessel, the *Duke of Portland*, in these waters.

"Farewell, vain world, for I have seen enough of thee,
I pay no further heed to what thou sayest of me;
Thy charmed or wrathful looks cause me no more alarm,
For now my mind's at rest and I have found peace and
    calm.

Fall not into those faults that in me thou hast known,
Tend thine own house, therein is ample to be done."[8]

Back at Port aux Français. "This might be of some interest to you," the *disker* says, handing me a message from Paris. I learn that Edgar Aubert de la Rüe, "a leading figure in the southern ocean lands," has just died in Lausanne at the age of ninety.

I thought he had died long ago. At the religious service held at Touffreville six months earlier, Father Bossière had asked us to pray for all the dead, from the Chevalier de Kerguelen onwards, who had made a name for themselves in the Desolation Islands. Aubert de la Rüe was among them.

He was the last man of the heroic age. He thought that the ultimate archives of the universe were hidden in this untouched land so far from the world. He insisted that "men respect this unique sanctuary in which France can take pride." A chain of mountains on the Gallieni Peninsula bears the name of Aubert de la Rüe, but it is the name of his wife Andrée, with whom he traveled through the archipelago.

A late afternoon ceremony outside Our Lady of the Winds. Captain Couesnon outlines the story of the Bossière brothers. About twenty men of the winter mission are there to take part in the unveiling of the plaque under a dark, threatening sky. It had poured with rain during the morning. Port aux Français is covered with puddles, which the howling wind hasn't managed to blow away. The plaque has been set in place not far from the grave of Moilimou Bedja, the Cormoran.

The Christmas Harbor *manip.* has been cancelled because of bad weather. I'll never see the Arch of Kerguelen.

There is the *Marion-Dufresne*, motionless against the sharp outline of the jagged edges of Mount Ross. It arrived during the night. Rust runs like blood down the sides of the big whale of a ship.

The ship weighs anchor. Water falls drop by drop from this dark dragon suddenly hauled away from its hunting among the grasses of the deep-sea meadows. The anchor looks wounded; it bears the scars of an underwater battle; it can bite. Seaweed clings to its long pointed teeth, which have plowed the ocean floor. And yet, the water makes it look limp, like someone almost suffocating.

I've taken refuge in my cabin at the moment of departure. I don't want to look back. I'll never see Kerguelen again. Through my porthole the sky rolls then disappears. "Then the sky receded as a scroll when it is rolled up." (Revelation)

Return to France. I discover that the Arch no longer exists. It was destroyed between 1909 and 1914. If I had read the account of Rallier du Baty's second voyage more carefully, I would have learned that all that remains of the Arch today are "two columns like the towers of Notre Dame."

Genthieu, August 1992

Endnotes

PART ONE

1. *Relation de deux voyages dans les mers australes* [Account of two voyages in the southern oceans], Paris, Knapen et fils, 1782.

2. French sailors go further and call the shank the shaft [*la verge*], and the ring at the top that holds the chain a little organ [*l'organeau*].

3. *Reflections on the Possible Advantages to Be Gained from France in the Southern Ocean.*

PART TWO

1. A map of the imaginary Land of Love showing the Lover how he must proceed, what places he must avoid (e.g. the Lake of Indifference), and those he must visit to succeed in his quest (e.g. Sincerity, Billet doux). From the seventeenth century précieux novel *Clélie* by Mlle de Scudéry. [Tr.]

2. In French the sheet anchor is called *l'ancre de miséricorde*, "the mercy anchor."

3. A map supposedly from the *Dauphine*, 1774. The name was never used.

4. The *loup-marin* or sea wolf is a term for a seal, sea lion, or sea elephant. [Tr.]

5. *The Journals of Captain James Cook. The Voyage of the Resolution and Discovery (1776–1780)*, ed. J. C. Beaglehole, Part One, CUP for the Hakluyt Society, 1967.

6. Cook had the following inscription written on the other side of the parchment before putting it back in a bottle: *Naves Resolution & Discovery/ de Rege Magnae Brittanie/ Decembris 1776.* [Tr.]

PART THREE

1. Benoît Heimermann, postcript to Raymond Rallier du Baty's *Adventures in Kerguelen.*

2. *Quotidien de la Réunion* [*Réunion Daily*], 1 August 1986.

3. The daily toll is reported to be up as much as 3,500 birds, or 1.2–2.3 million in a year (Michel Pascal in the review *Mammalia*).

4. A Breton word meaning *blue.* Perhaps a reference to the color of the slate. [Tr.]

5. Inhabitants of part of Canada then called Nouvelle-France, now Nova Scotia and part of New Brunswick, ceded to England in 1713. [Tr.]

6. Preface to *La Ridondaine*, by Guillemette Marrier (Plon, 1945).

7. Campaign of Franco-Soviet launches (FUSOV). Twenty M100 rockets were launched in the Courbet Peninsula in 1974.

8. *Ordenburgen* (Castles of the Order) were residential colleges for the training of a Nazi élite. [Tr.]

9. Cf. *Les Allemands aux Kerguelen durant la Deuxième Guerre mondiale* [*The Germans on Kerguelen during the Second World War*], by Gracie Delépine, *TAAF Revue* no. 26, 1964. The details contained in this passage a largely taken from this article.

10. Quoted by Auguste Dupouy in *Le Breton Yves de Kerguelen* [*Yves de Kerguelen, The Breton*].

PART FOUR

1. A naïve search for an improbable adventure, like something out of Alphonse Daudet's comic novel *Les Aventures prodigieuses de Tartarin de Tarascon* (1872). [Tr.]

2. French writer Georges Courteline (1858–1929), best known for his acute and sometimes bitter satire. [Tr.]

3. Roger Vercel.

4. Régis Debray, *Christophe Colomb, le visiteur de l'aube* [*Christopher Columbus, the Dawn Visitor*], La Différence, 1992.

5. There has been noticeable warming in Kerguelen since the 30s (1.5°). This accelerated enormously in the eighties (a very rapid recession of the Diosaz glacier, which has lost more than two miles).

6. Benoît Heimermann, op. cit.

7. Léon Ménager's journal, 1929 (extract from *Le Petit Havre*).

8. This is a rendering from the author's French transcription, as the original epitaph in English is unavailable. [Tr.]

Bibliography

For the history, geology, fauna and flora of Kerguelen, I have consulted the following works:

Couesnon (Pierre), *Histoire postale des Kerguelen*, Éditions Bertrand Sinais, 1989 (a new edition in preparation at time of writing).

Brossard (Amiral de), *Kerguelen*, 2 vols, Éditions France-Empire, 1970.

Duchêne (Jean-Claude), *Kerguelen, recherches au bout du monde*, TAAF [Terres australes et antarctiques françaises], 1989.

Commission territoriale de toponymie [Territorial Toponymy Commission] with the participation of Gracie Delépine, *Toponymie des Terres australes*, 1973.

Delépine (Gracie), articles in the *Revue TAAF* (nos 26, 42-43, 54, 68-69).

Un naufragé célèbre aux îles Kerguelen: John Nunn (1825-1829), trans. J. Beaugé (published in the *Revue TAAF* (nos 28, 29, 30, 31, 32, 33). First edition William Edward Painter, London, 1850.

Aubert de la Rüe (Edgar), *Terres françaises inconnues*, Société parisienne d'éditon, 1930.

Deux ans aux îles de la Désolation, Julliard, 1954.

Peau (Étienne), *Mission aux îles Kerguelen (1923-1924)*, unpublished.

Martin-Allanic (J.-E.), *Bougainville navigateur et les découvertes de son temps*, 2 vols, PUF, 1964.

Dupouy (Auguste), *Le Breton Yves de Kerguelen*, La Renaissance du Livre, 1929.

Rallier du Baty (Raymond), *Aventures aux Kerguelen.*

Most of these works are now out of print. The last work mentioned may be obtained from Éditions Maritimes et d'Outremer (1991).

Alain Boulaire, who is working on Yves de Kerguelen's trial, has given me guidance and advice. I have consulted the Navy archives in Brest, where all the trial documents are located (Ms 171), as well as Kerguelen's reports and memoranda in the National Archives:

Réflexions sur les avantages que peut procurer la France australe.

Mémoire sur l'établissement d'une colonie dans la France australe (Mar. B-4-317).